HOW TO BE A
Coder

Written by
Kiki Prottsman

Project editor Olivia Stanford
Project art editor Emma Hobson
Additional editorial Marie Greenwood,
Seeta Parmar, Jolyon Goddard
Design assistant Xiao Lin
Additional design Charlotte Jennings, Jaileen Kaur
US Senior editor Shannon Beatty
US Editor Margaret Parrish
Illustrations Mark Ruffle, Katie Knutton
DTP designer Mrinmoy Mazumdar
Senior picture researcher Sumedha Chopra
Jacket co-ordinator Issy Walsh
Senior jacket designer Elle Ward
Managing editor Laura Gilbert
Managing art editor Diane Peyton Jones
Pre-production producer Dragana Puvacic
Senior producer Ena Matagic
Creative director Helen Senior
Publishing director Sarah Larter

Consultant Sway Grantham

First American Edition, 2019
Published in the United States by DK Publishing
1450 Broadway, Suite 801, New York, NY 10018

A catalog record for this book
is available from the Library of Congress.
ISBN 978-1-4654-7881-8

DK books are available at special discounts when purchased
in bulk for sales promotions, premiums, fund-raising, or educational use.
For details, contact: DK Publishing Special Markets,
1450 Broadway, Suite 801, New York, NY 10018
SpecialSales@dk.com

Printed and bound in China

A WORLD OF IDEAS:
SEE ALL THERE IS TO KNOW

www.dk.com

Contents

4 How the book works
6 Getting ready

① Crafty coding

10 Origami algorithm
14 Ada Lovelace
16 Paper pixels
18 Scavenger hunt program
20 Debugging drawings
22 Loopy orchestra
24 Creative outlines
26 Games
28 Illustration collaboration
30 Persistence pointing
32 Conditional questions
34 The if/else dance
36 Alan Turing
38 Balloon events
40 Input/output recipe
44 Hardware
46 Catch me collisions
48 Variable paper chain
50 Fortune-teller function
54 Katherine Johnson
56 Parameter path
58 Decompose a castle
62 Pattern matching creepy-crawlies
64 Abstraction story
66 Remixing rhymes
68 The internet

2 Computer coding

72 Getting Scratch
74 Using Scratch
76 Coding in Scratch
78 Sprites
80 Algorithms
84 Programming languages
86 Coding programs
88 Debugging
90 Loops
92 Creativity
94 Collaboration
96 Persistence
98 Conditionals
100 If/else
102 Events
104 Input/output
106 Collisions
108 Variables
110 Satoru Iwata
112 Functions
114 Functions with parameters
116 Decomposition
120 Pattern matching
122 Abstraction
124 Bill Gates
126 Remixing
130 Minicomputers
132 micro:bit

135 Answers
136 Did you know?
138 Glossary
140 Index
144 Acknowledgments

Repeat 3 times

Strum

Rest

Strum

Rest

How the book works

In *How to be a Coder,* you will learn how to think and act like a coder. The book is full of fun activities that can be done at home, as well as simple programs, and information on some of the most famous coders of all time.

Awesome activities

Look in the beginning of the book to find exciting offline activities that let you discover the ideas that are important to coding. These examples don't require a computer, but they will help you prepare to write programs.

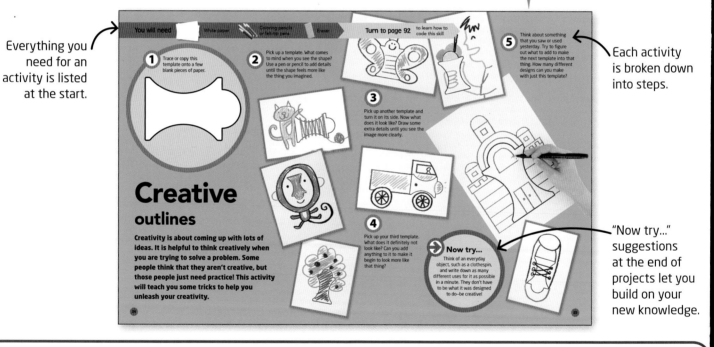

Everything you need for an activity is listed at the start.

Each activity is broken down into steps.

"Now try..." suggestions at the end of projects let you build on your new knowledge.

Safety first

All of the projects in this book should be done with care. If you see this symbol at the top of a page, it means that you will need an adult to help you with the activity.

Be particularly careful when:
- you are using sharp objects, such as scissors;
- you are running around with friends;
- you are handling hot food;
- you are outside—always tell an adult what you are doing.

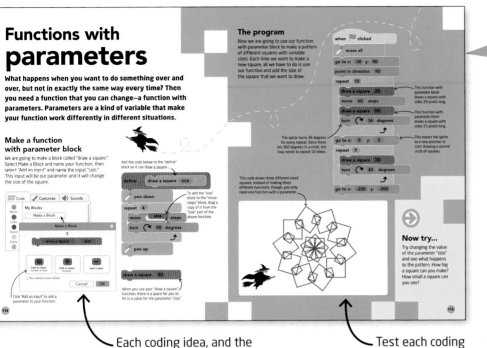

Each coding idea, and the blocks needed to code it, are explained simply.

Test each coding concept using the provided program.

Cool coding

Building your own code is exciting, but it can be tricky. This book will give you activities and examples for each coding idea so that you can learn how to use your new skills to make code of your own!

Top topics

Learn about some of the key coding topics, such as hardware, the internet, and programming languages. These will help you understand the craft and coding projects.

Great coders

Anyone can learn how to code, and this book will show you the people who have made a difference in the world with their coding skills.

Getting ready

You can do many of the projects in this book right away. Most of the craft projects can be done with items you have at home and the coding projects just need a computer and an internet connection.

A keyboard is essential for coders to write their code with.

Learning to code is all about solving problems.

What is a coder?

A coder is a person who writes instructions, or code, to make computers work. Some coders program for a living and others program for fun. You don't have to program every day to be a coder. However, just like with drawing or playing the piano, you will get better with practice!

You don't need a complicated computer to start coding. Minicomputers like this can also be used.

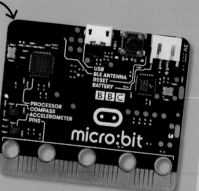

micro:bit

USB
BLE ANTENNA
RESET
BATTERY

BBC

PROCESSOR
COMPASS
ACCELEROMETER
PINS

Get your pencil ready. It can be helpful to draw or write problems out before you start to code.

Thinking like a coder

Coders have all kinds of talents. One thing that most coders share, however, is a love of problem-solving. If you want to think like a coder, keep these things in mind:

1 Coders think ahead. Programs can be complicated, so it is helpful to know what you want at the start.

2 Coders break things down. By taking one piece of a plan at a time, you can try different things without changing the rest of your program.

3 Coders are imaginative. Start by imagining what your code will do before you make it. This will help you think of different types of program to create.

4 Coders are careful. One little mistake can keep your whole program from working, so always check your code twice.

5 Coders solve mysteries. When something is not right, see if you can find any clues about what went wrong.

6 Coders are persistent. Decide to try again. Try over and over. If you quit too soon, it will be hard to learn anything new.

7 Coders don't give up. If something doesn't work out, don't worry. Everyone makes mistakes! You can still end up with something you're proud of in the end.

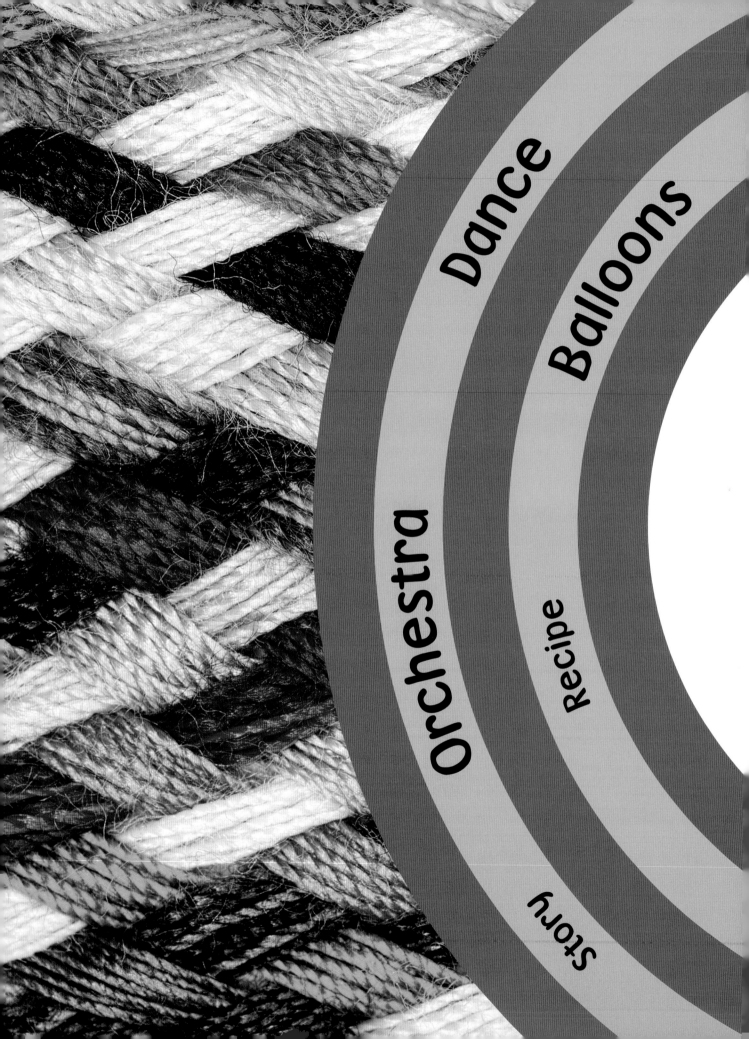

Dance

Balloons

Orchestra

Recipe

Story

Crafty coding

The ideas that computer scientists use in coding can be found everywhere. In this chapter, you will see them in arts, crafts, recipes, and games! Try these activities to get familiar with the concepts that coders use every day.

Paper chain

Origami

Rhymes

Outlines

Questions

Using paper that is colorful or patterned on one side will help you to follow the steps of the algorithm.

1 Begin with a rectangular piece of paper—letter size works well. To start, fold your paper in half, from top to bottom.

2 Fold the paper in half again, from left to right, and press firmly along the fold. Then unfold it.

Origami algorithm

An algorithm is a list of steps that tells you what to do. A recipe is an algorithm and sheet music is an algorithm, too. Algorithms are the first step in planning a computer program. Did you know that you can follow an algorithm to make an origami boat?

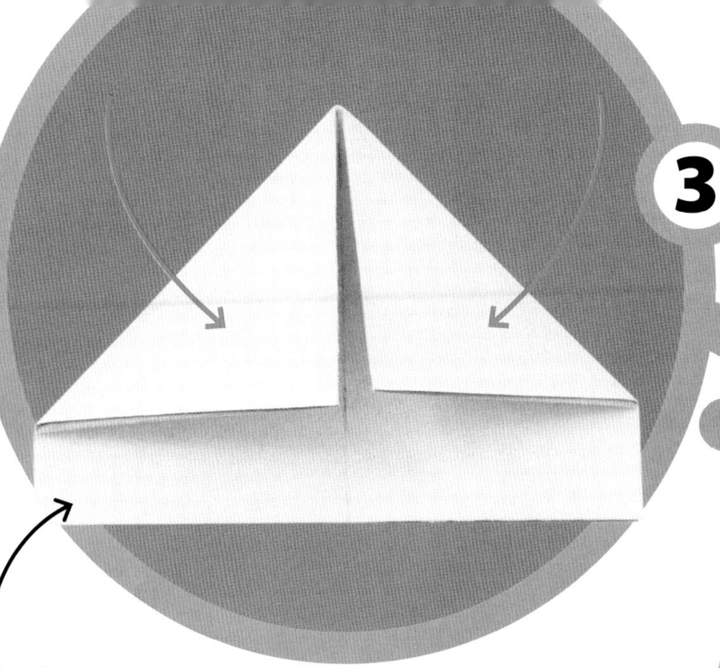

3 Next, fold the top-left corner toward the center line, then fold the top-right corner down to meet it. This will create a triangle with a rectangle at the bottom.

It is important to follow the steps of an algorithm in the right order, or it won't work properly.

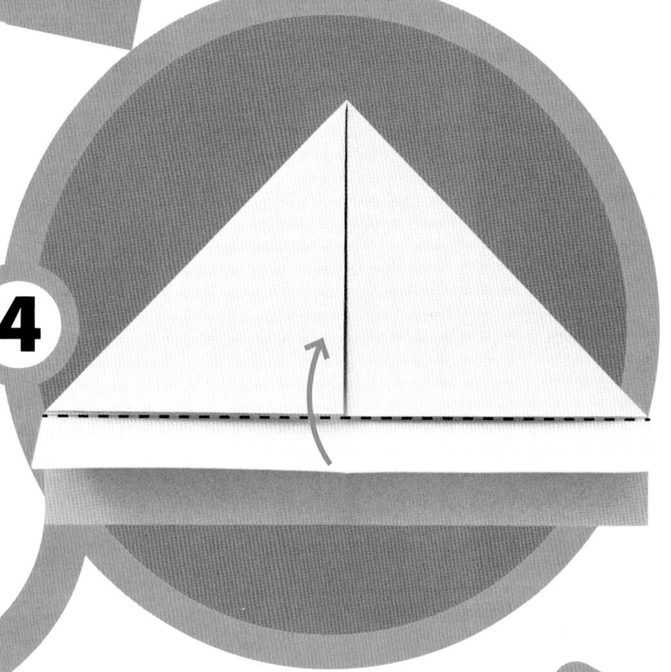

The bottom rectangle will be made of two sheets of paper. Fold the upper piece up, over the base of triangle along the line where they meet.

4

5 Tuck the corners that stick out over the triangle behind it, and flip the whole thing over.

Fold the remaining sheet of the rectangle up along the line where it meets the triangle.

You're already halfway through the origami algorithm!

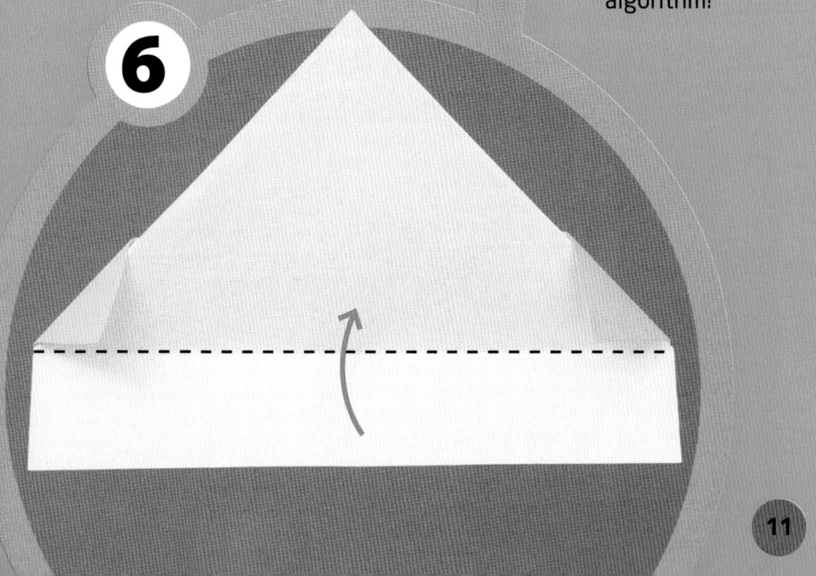

6

7

The next part is a bit tricky. Put your fingers inside the pocket made by the two halves of the triangle and open it out, pushing the ends together so it folds into a diamond.

8

The bottom half of the diamond will be made of two halves. Fold the top half up to meet the top of the diamond, then turn the whole thing over and fold the second half up as well. This will create a triangle.

Each step of making this origami boat is another step in the algorithm.

9

As in step 7, put your fingers inside the two halves of the triangle and open it out, pushing the ends together so it folds into a diamond.

10 For the final step, take the top loose points of the diamond and pull them outward to make your boat. The algorithm is complete.

Ahoy!

Ada Lovelace

Mathematician • Born 1815
• From the United Kingdom

Ada Lovelace was the daughter of the famous poet Lord Byron. Though her mother discouraged her from studying poetry, Lovelace found an outlet for her imagination in mathematics and technology. She believed both could change the future.

Charles Babbage

Lovelace met inventor Charles Babbage when she was 17, and they became good friends. He had designed the "analytical engine"—a mechanical machine that could be programmed to solve tricky calculations. The machine was not built in his lifetime, but Lovelace was still fascinated with its potential uses.

The analytical engine was an early computer—it could be programmed and had memory to store information.

Analytical engine

Lovelace translated an article about the analytical engine from French into English. She added her own thoughts to the pages, and among those notes were plans for how the machine could be programmed. Some consider these notes to be the first computer algorithm—making Lovelace the first published computer coder.

To tell the engine what to do, a series of cards with holes punched into them would be inserted into the machine.

Early life

A scientist from a very early age, Lovelace wrote to her mother at 12 that she had visions of creating a mechanical flying horse with wings so large that it would be capable of carrying a person on its back!

Inspiration

Lovelace's ideas about the analytical engine inspired future programmers. Alan Turing, who designed early computers, wrote about her article over 100 years later. Every second Tuesday of October she is celebrated on Ada Lovelace Day.

Paper pixels

Pixels are the tiny squares of colored light that make up your screen. If you zoom in on an image on a computer, you'll see that it's actually made up of many single-colored blocks. Try following these steps to make a pixel image with paper!

1

Use a ruler to divide two different-colored square pieces of paper into 8 by 8 grids. We've used green and yellow paper.

2

Cut along the lines using safety scissors so you end up with 64 paper pixels of each color.

3

Next, grab the piece of white paper. It should be the same size as the pieces of colored paper. Again, draw an 8 by 8 grid on it—but don't cut it up.

4

Follow the instructions to fill the grid in and reveal a mystery picture. To figure out which spot each paper pixel goes in, you need to assign a code to the columns and rows. Here, the letters tell you which column to use and the numbers tell you which row. Once you've found the right square, glue the correct colored pixel there.

Instructions

Fill in the following squares with your paper pixels:

Yellow: B5, C6, D7, E6, F5

Green: A4, B3, B4, C2, C3, C4, C5, D3, D4, D5, D6, E2, E3, E4, E5, F3, F4, G5, G6, H6

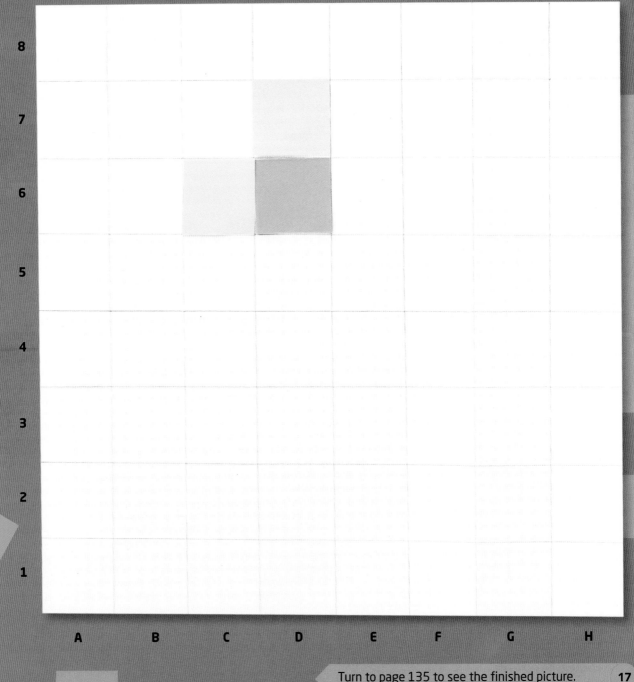

Scavenger hunt program

A program is an algorithm, or set of instructions, that has been written in a special code that a machine can read. You can make up your own code and write a program with it to help a friend solve a scavenger hunt!

Once you and your frien[d] have decided on your symbols get your friend to look away or step out of the room

2

1

First, you and your friend should decide on a set of 5-10 coded symbols that stand for the actions that you are allowed to take to find the treasure. These can be anything that will remind you of what they mean—for example, you might want to use an arrow to mean "Take a step forward." Here are some examples you can use:

Crouch down   **Look underneath**   **R**
                                                          Turn right

Move forward 3 steps   **Pick it up**   **L**
                                                       Turn left

18

Turn to page 86 to learn how to code this skill

3 Hide your objects around the room, and remember where they are—you will need to be able to use your symbols to guide your friend to their locations.

4 Pick a starting point and use your symbols to write out a program for your friend to follow. You might have to practice to figure out how many steps they will need to take, or which way to turn.

5 Guide your friend to the starting point, give them the program, and watch them go! Did your code work? How many of the items were they able to find?

Debugging drawings

Debugging is an important part of coding. It is easy to make errors when translating algorithms into code. This activity will help you find and fix the mistakes, or "bugs," in the instructions for drawing a shark.

1 Fold your paper in half the long way three times in a row, then open the paper back up. Next, fold the piece of paper in half the other way three times in a row and then open it back up again. You now have a grid of fold lines for the rest of the activity!

Like connect the dots, this activity is played by drawing lines from one location to another. Each fold line is given a number so you know where to draw. Start by putting your pencil down at the corner that represents 0 squares over and 2 squares up.

2

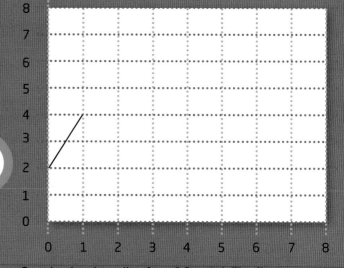

Start by drawing a line from 0,2 to 1,4. The first number represents the lines going across and the second number represents the lines up and down.

Turn to page 88 to learn how to code this skill

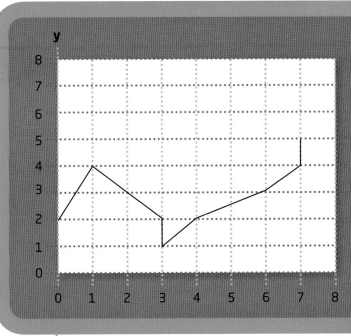

3 Follow the directions in the boxes and you will see a shark start to appear!

Go down diagonally to 3,2. Then go straight down to 3,1. Next go up diagonally to 4,2, then 6,3, and again to 7,4. Now go straight up to 7,5.

Oh, no! Some of the instructions in this box are not right! Can you find and fix the bugs in the numbers to make the picture look like a shark?

If you're having trouble finding the errors, take a look at the shark below and see how you can change the instructions to match the shape.

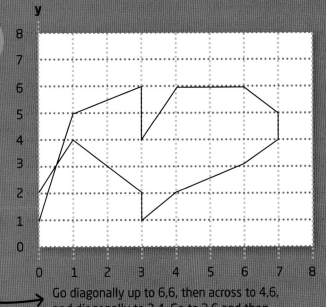

4

Go diagonally up to 6,6, then across to 4,6, and diagonally to 3,4. Go to 3,6 and then diagonally down to 1,5. Finish at 0, 1.

5 Once you've fixed the shark you can color it in. Don't forget to add the details of its eye, gills, and teeth!

Turn to page 135 to check the answer.

Give a friend the bowl and spoons to use as a drum.

2

Choose a third friend to be the singer. If only two friends are playing, someone can sing while they play an instrument.

3

Stretch the rubber bands around the plastic tub. Make sure they are loose enough that you can grab and pull them to make noise, but not so loose that they fall off.

1 ⚠

Loopy orchestra

Repeat loops are one of the most helpful things in all of programming! Without loops, you'd have to write each line of code out separately, even if you wanted to do the exact same thing 100 times. Instead, you can add a loop around the instructions that you want repeated for as many times as you like. You can even use loops to make music!

Turn to page 90 to learn how to code this skill

Repeat 3 times

Tap

Rest

Tap

Rest

4 Each instrument will have its own set of instructions that look something like this. The loop box around them tells you how many times to repeat the instructions inside.

5

Now, play the loops below. You need to make sure that you all play your parts on the same beat for each count of four. How did it go? Change the instructions inside the loops to change the music!

The loop box tells you to repeat the instructions inside it three times, then stop.

Repeat 3 times

Sing "Beepop"

Sing "Beep"

Sing "Beep"

Sing "Beep"

Repeat 3 times

Tap

Tap

Tap

Rest

Repeat 3 times

Strum

Rest

Strum

Rest

1 Trace or copy this template onto a few blank pieces of paper.

2 Pick up a template. What comes to mind when you see the shape? Use a pen or pencil to add details until the shape feels more like the thing you imagined.

Creative
outlines

Creativity is about coming up with lots of ideas. It is helpful to think creatively when you are trying to solve a problem. Some people think that they aren't creative, but those people just need practice! This activity will teach you some tricks to help you unleash your creativity.

Turn to page 92

to learn how to code this skill

5 Think about something that you saw or used yesterday. Try to figure out what to add to make the next template into that thing. How many different designs can you make with just this template?

3

Pick up another template and turn it on its side. Now what does it look like? Draw some extra details until you see the image more clearly.

4

Pick up your third template. What does it definitely not look like? Can you add anything to it to make it begin to look more like that thing?

Now try...

Think of an everyday object, such as a clothespin, and write down as many different uses for it as possible in a minute. They don't have to be what it was designed to do—be creative!

Games

People might decide to learn to code because they want to make games. Computer games are a lot of fun and very popular. Games can be played on your own or with friends. Increasingly, programmers have put a lot of work into creating gaming experiences that are easy to use and feel a lot like real life.

Virtual reality

In virtual reality games, you take part in an imaginary world. A headset with a screen makes you feel like you're inside the game. Augmented reality games show you the world around you but add virtual objects that you can play with.

Some multiplayer games can be played over the internet with an adult's permission.

Some controllers make you feel like you're playing a musical instrument.

Special controllers

To help players feel more connected to an activity, some games use special controllers that look like musical instruments, rackets, steering wheels, or even magic wands.

Mobile gaming

Mobile games are games you can play anywhere. They used to be only played on handheld consoles, but today's mobile games are usually played on a smartphone. Mobile games are often simple to play, which makes them very popular among people of all ages.

Online gaming

You need an internet connection to play games online. Some games can be played by yourself, while others need two or three players. There are some online games that can be played with hundreds of people from all around the world.

Games consoles

Consoles are special computers designed to run games. Popular consoles include Sony PlayStation, Nintendo Switch, and Microsoft Xbox. Many games are made especially for consoles. They can be very complex and may come with special controllers.

Illustration collaboration

Most coders work in teams. Working with other people on a project is called collaboration. It helps you create things that you might not have thought of on your own. Try drawing a picture with friends and see what different ideas you come up with!

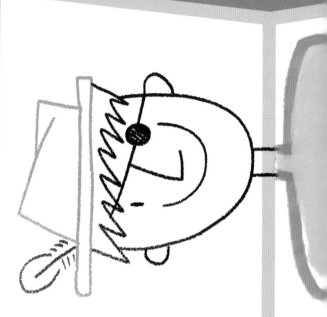

1

Before you begin, fold a piece of paper in half lengthwise, then in half again in the same direction. Open it out and you should have four equal rectangles.

2

First, draw a head, but don't let your friends see what you've drawn. Make sure the neck crosses the first fold to give the next artist something to connect the body to. Then fold your section back to hide it and pass it to the next person.

Turn to page 94 to learn how to code this skill

Each artist should draw a little over the bottom crease to give the next person a place to start.

Remember to fold each section back so the other artists can't see what you've drawn until the end.

Now try...

Instead of a drawing, why not try a collaborative story? Write down one sentence on a piece of paper and then pass it to a friend to write the next sentence. Keep going for as long as you can!

3

The next artist should draw the top half of the body. Again, make sure the lines for the body and arms cross the fold so the next artist can see them once that section has been folded back.

4

Start from where the second artist left off and add the hands and hips. You can start the legs for the last artist, too.

5

Finish off the drawing with the legs and feet. Once the last artist has finished, unfold the paper and see what you have created together!

Persistence
pointing

Learning to do something difficult means trying again and again until you finally get it right. Working hard to succeed at something that you've failed at several times is called persistence, and you'll need it when you're learning to program.

3 Switch both hands to the opposite sign at the same time.

After you've counted to three, switch your finger and thumb instantly.

2 Count to three.

Make sure you don't have your thumb up on your pointing hand.

1 Give the "thumbs-up" sign with your left hand while pointing forward with your right hand.

5 Once you can repeat the switch five times without messing up, you win! You might need to practice a few times until you can master switching quickly. Keep persisting!

1... 2... 3...

1... 2... 3...

4 If at any time you have your thumb up and finger pointing on the same hand, you lose and must begin again.

Conditional questions

A conditional is a piece of code that checks if a statement is true or false. When you see a conditional, it's like your program is asking a yes-or-no question. If the answer is yes, then the statement is true. You can use conditionals to figure out what mystery person or object your friend has chosen for you.

Choose a statement that can either be true or false to ask your friend, to help you figure out which person or thing they have chosen for you.

3

I'm alive?

1

Together with your friend, choose a category such as plants, animals, or famous people.

2

Hmmm... OK, I've got it.

Have your friend choose someone or something from that category that you will be—but they shouldn't tell you what it is!

4 Your friend will either answer with "True" or "False."

Only move on to your next statement once you have found out if your current statement is true or false.

False!

True!

Repeat steps 3 and 4 up to 20 times. If you guess what your friend was thinking before the 20th question, you win! **5**

"We choose the category water."

"OK, I've got it!"

"I'm alive?"

"False."

"I can float?"

"True."

"I'm a boat?"

"True! You win!"

I won!

The if/else dance

An if/else statement is a type of conditional that runs one set of code if something is true and another set of code if it is false. The moves of the if/else dance change depending on if certain statements about the time, date, or weather are true or false.

If the time is "a.m.," use the top half of the chart. Else, use the bottom half.

What day of the week is it? If it's a weekday, use the right half of the page. Else, use the left.

Is it sunny outside? If it is, do the dance backward! Else, do it forward (top to bottom).

1

If it's Monday to Friday, you do one of the dances on the right-hand side of the chart. Else, if it's Saturday or Sunday, do one of the dances on the left.

If the time is a.m.

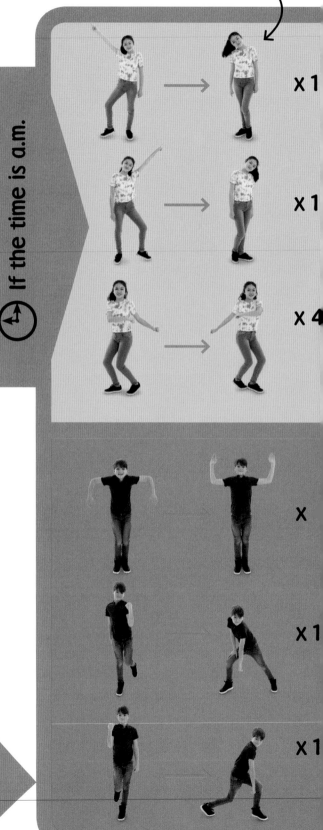

x 1

x 1

x 4

X

x 1

x 1

To do this dance right, you have a lot of statements to check! You'll need to know the time, what day of the week it is, and what the weather is like to figure out what dance you should do.

to learn how to
code this skill

📅 If today is a weekday

Let's say it's 8:00 a.m. on Monday. Since it is the morning, you use the top half of the chart, and because it's a weekday, you use the right-hand box.

2

3

Now check the weather. If it is raining, do the moves forward (top to bottom), else if it is sunny, do them backward. Here's the dance that you'd do on a rainy Monday morning!

Alan Turing

Mathematician • Born 1912 • From the United Kingdom

Alan Turing is known as the father of computer science. Having always been fond of numbers, he was very interested in problem-solving. Turing helped to win World War II by working to read coded enemy messages.

Turing machines

Turing studied math at the University of Cambridge. After graduating, he invented the concept of "Turing machines." A Turing machine uses a program to solve mathematical problems using a strip of paper. Although he never built one, this simple machine is believed to be able to solve any problem that a modern-day computer could!

Checkmate

Turing helped create Turochamp, the first program that could play chess against a human. Unfortunately, there wasn't a computer that could yet run the program, so he had to settle for being the computer himself and running the program with a pencil and paper!

Cracking the code

During World War II, Turing helped make a device, called the Bombe, that decoded the secret messages created by the German's Enigma machine. Being able to read enemy messages helped the Allies to win the war.

The Bombe decoded German messages by testing every possible combination of letters.

Artificial intelligence

In order to test how intelligent a machine is, Turing suggested a written quiz. A person would ask a computer that they couldn't see questions and try to tell if it was a computer or a human. This quiz is known as a "Turing test."

The Enigma machine changed all the letters of a message into different letters, and back again, so only someone with an Enigma machine could read them.

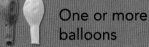
Whoever has the balloons should play around with them to see what events get a reaction from the other person. Here are some examples of balloon events to try:

Shake the balloon

Drop the balloon

Hug the balloon

Poke the balloon

The person doing the actions needs to decide in their head what they will do when certain events happen to the balloons. Choose one action for each different balloon event. Here are some example actions:

Run on the spot

Clap

Wave

Jump

Balloon events

Events are actions that interrupt a program and make something happen. If you want to have the score in your video game change when the main character gets hit by a meteor, then you will need an event! Here, the game is to play with balloons and try to guess what event your friend is reacting to.

1 First, decide who will play with the balloons and who will do the actions. The goal is for the person playing with the balloons to figure out which balloon events cause the other player to do certain actions.

2 To play, start trying different events with the balloons. If the other player sees an event that matches their idea for an action, they should do it. For example, hugging a balloon might make the other player clap their hands.

to learn how to code this skill

3 Once you have figured out the action for each different balloon event, move on to the next one.

Once you think you've figured out an event that gets a reaction, repeat it to see if the other player does the same thing again.

Keep trying different events with the balloons to see what gets a reaction. What happens if you throw a balloon in the air?

4

5

Once the person with the balloons has figured out what all the event-action combinations are, it's time to switch roles!

| You will need | | Apron | | Two mixing bowls | Table knife | | Pitcher |
| Ingredients | | 1¾ cups flour | Pinch of salt | | 3½ tbsp butter | | ½ cup grated cheese |

Input/output recipe

Input is the information you give to a computer, such as the text you type on a keyboard, and output is the information the computer gives you, such as what appears on the screen. In this recipe you can use different ingredients (the inputs) to make two different types of biscuit (the outputs)!

Ask an adult to preheat the oven to 425°F/220°C. Then put the flour, salt, and butter into a mixing bowl. Carefully use a table knife to cut the butter into small cubes.

Work the butter into the flour with your fingers until the whole mixture looks like a bowl of bread crumbs. Now put half of the mixture into a new bowl and get ready to add the different inputs.

1 ⚠️

2

The different inputs will give you two different types of biscuit that taste and look very different!

If the mixture is too wet you can add a little more flour.

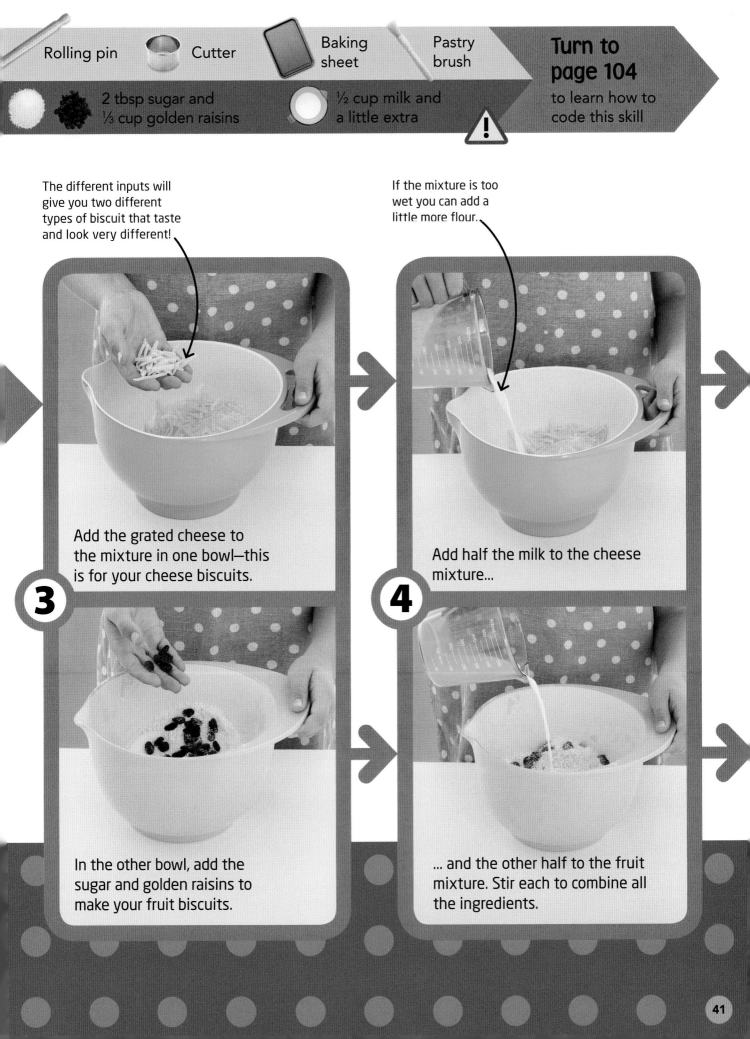

3 Add the grated cheese to the mixture in one bowl—this is for your cheese biscuits.

In the other bowl, add the sugar and golden raisins to make your fruit biscuits.

4 Add half the milk to the cheese mixture...

... and the other half to the fruit mixture. Stir each to combine all the ingredients.

Knead both mixtures with your hands until they are smooth balls of dough. Use a rolling pin—or your hands—to flatten both doughs until they are about 1 in (2 cm) thick.

Use a 2 in (6 cm) pastry cutter to cut out your biscuits. There should be enough dough for at least six biscuits of each flavor.

5

6

7 Space the biscuits out on a baking sheet, then brush the tops with milk using a pastry brush. Ask an adult to put them in the oven and bake them for 12 to 15 minutes, until they are golden brown.

8

Once they have cooled, you can enjoy your biscuits! Do you see how the different outputs were affected by the different inputs you put in?

Hardware

Hardware is any part of a computer that you can touch. Most pieces of hardware, such as a keyboard, come with little bits of code, called drivers, that help the computer know what to do with them. Different types of hardware can be used to input or output information or to help the computer run.

Computer

A computer is a machine built from various pieces of hardware, some of which you can see, and some which are found inside it. PCs are computers, but so are many other devices, such as smartphones.

A keyboard is used to input words and numbers, as well as to control the computer.

Central processing unit

The central processing unit (CPU) is like the brain of the computer. This is where all of the most important decisions are made. The CPU sends and receives information, makes calculations, and carries out instructions.

Today's CPUs have several "cores." This lets one CPU process multiple instructions at a time.

Graphics card

A graphics card handles the difficult calculations that go with displaying pictures and images on the screen. Some cards have their own graphics processing unit (GPU) to reduce the amount of work the CPU has to do.

Graphics cards connect directly to the motherboard.

RAM

RAM stands for "random access memory." It acts as lightning-fast storage that your computer can use to save information when the CPU gets full.

Information is stored on tiny devices called memory chips.

A monitor, or screen, lets you see what's happening.

A speaker changes audio signals into sound.

The mouse lets you interact with the computer.

How a computer works

A computer takes input from a user or sensor, processes it—often using a central processing unit—and then is able to store the result in its memory or output it.

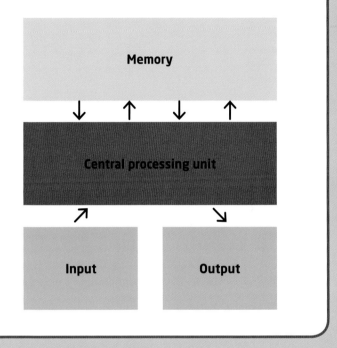

Memory

Central processing unit

Input

Output

Hard drive

The hard drive is the part of the computer where information is stored. Some hard drives have a spinning disk inside, while others are more like a giant store of RAM.

Motherboard

The motherboard is the piece of hardware that connects all of the other parts together. It's the main connection point for a computer's cards, chips, and cables.

Some motherboards include a fan to keep the CPU cool.

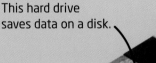

This hard drive saves data on a disk.

The RAM connects straight to the motherboard, too.

These slots allow you to connect other devices.

Catch me collisions

In coding, collisions happen when two or more things touch. They let characters pick up objects in video games and they stop your cursor when it hits the edge of your screen. In this activity, you have to avoid colliding with the catcher or you'll be stuck!

When the catcher catches, o "collides" with, a player, that playe should freeze with their arms out

2

Make sure you collide gently with your friends! You don't want to hurt them.

1

Decide what part of the room or yard is your playing zone. Choose someone to be the "catcher" and have them stand in the center. Everyone else should stand at the edges. When the catcher shouts "GO!" everyone should start running around.

GO!

Another player can free a frozen player by touching them on the shoulder. Then the frozen player can start running again.

3

The game is over when all players except the catcher are frozen in place.

4

Variable paper chain

Variables allow parts of a program to change, even while it is running. All you have to do is choose a word to hold the place of the part that will change—this word is your variable.

Cut paper to length: dieRoll + 5 in (12 cm)

Tape paper into circle

Repeat 15 times

Cut new strip: dieRoll + 5 in (12 cm)

Hook paper strip through the end of the last link and tape closed

Variable algorithm

This algorithm shows you how to make a paper chain with different-sized links. It contains a variable called "dieRoll." Whenever you see it, you roll a die and use the number that you rolled in place of the variable. This means the algorithm can change depending on the value you roll.

Start by cutting a piece of paper into strips along its full length, each about 1 in (3 cm) wide. You can use a few different colors of paper.

1

Turn to page 108 to learn how to code this skill

3

Keep running the algorithm until you have made at least 16 links. Add each new strip to the chain by looping it through the link before and taping it closed.

4

Once you have run the whole algorithm, you will have your finished variable paper chain!

Now you can run the algorithm. Take the first strip and roll the die. Add the value you get to 5 in (12 cm) and cut the strip to that length. For example, if you roll a 5, cut the strip to 10 in (25 cm) long. Tape this first strip into a circle. Repeat the instructions in the loop box to add more links to the chain.

2

Your paper chain will look different every time you run the algorithm because of the variable.

You will need

Square piece
of white paper

Felt-tip
pens

Turn to page 112

Fortune-teller function

A function is a set of instructions that you give a name. You only have to code your function once, then you can use it over and over again! Use the function below to make a paper fortune-teller to answer your questions.

Folding algorithm

Follow this algorithm to create a paper fortune-teller. Can you spot the function? You can look back at the instructions inside the function to see what to do.

1	Repeat 2 times
	Fold in half
	Undo
	Rotate 90°
2	Fold and turn
	Turn paper over
3	Fold and turn
	Turn paper over
4	Fold in half

Whenever the instructions say "Fold and turn," look at the function definition on the left to see what to do!

Folding function

This function tells you to fold a corner to the center of the paper, then rotate the paper 90 degrees. The "repeat" on the outside lets you know to do that four times.

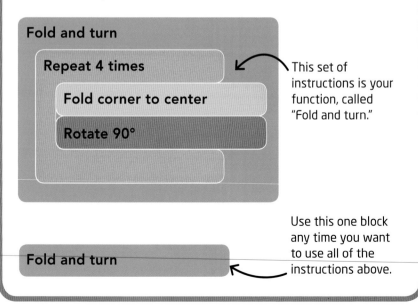

Fold and turn

   Repeat 4 times

      Fold corner to center

      Rotate 90°

This set of instructions is your function, called "Fold and turn."

Fold and turn

Use this one block any time you want to use all of the instructions above.

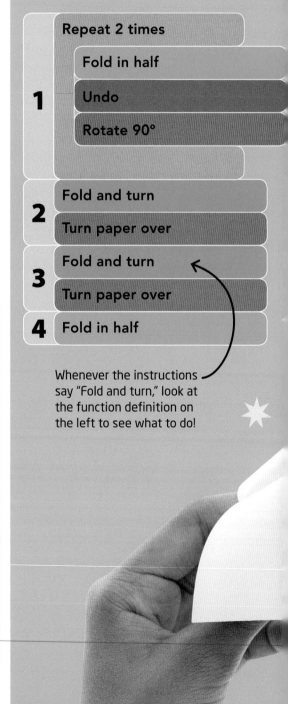

o learn how to
ode this skill

1

2

3

Once you have finished folding, you will need to put your fingers inside the folds and push them together to create the fortune-teller.

4

Turn over to find out how to use your fortune-teller.

Filling in your fortune-teller

Follow this simple guide to fill in your fortune-teller. The answers on the inner triangles will be the answers to your questions.

The four corners should all be filled in with different, bold colors.

The triangles that touch the corners need to have numbers 1–8 in them.

Each of the triangles that touches a number should hold a fortune!

How to use your fortune-teller

Now that the hard work is done, it's time to have some fun! Find a friend and follow the steps to find their fortune. It's like a fortune algorithm!

1 Have your friend think of a yes-or-no question. Then let them choose a color from the outside of the fortune-teller.

2 Go back and forth between opening the fortune-teller outward and side to side until you have spelled out all of the letters in the color that they chose.

Go back and forth between
opening the fortune-teller
outward and side to side
until you have counted
to that number.

4

3

However your fortune-
teller ends up, have your
friend choose one of the
numbers that is showing.

5

Have your friend choose
another number from inside.
Open the flap with that
number on it to reveal the
answer to their question!

Katherine Johnson

Mathematician • Born in 1918
• From the United States

Johnson is a brilliant mathematician who helped to figure out the flight paths of early spacecraft. She worked for the American space agency NACA, which later became NASA. Her drive helped her become one of the first women allowed to go to secret government meetings.

John Glenn blasted off into space on February 20, 1962, in the Friendship 7 spacecraft.

Blast off!

In 1962, John Glenn became the first person to orbit the Earth. The path his spacecraft followed was calculated by electronic machines. However, John, uncomfortable with the new technology, asked for Johnson to double-check the numbers by hand.

Human computer

Back in 1952, before digital computers, the word "computer" was used as a job title. Human computers were intelligent people like Johnson who figured out, or "computed," tricky math problems.

Moon landing

Johnson's calculations were so accurate that NASA often asked her to confirm the results coming from their expensive electronic computers. Her work contributed to the Apollo 11 mission in 1969, which resulted in the world watching as the first astronauts walked on the moon.

Buzz Aldrin was the second person to walk on the moon, after Neil Armstrong, who took this picture.

Counting everything

Even as a child, Johnson loved numbers. She counted everything, from the number of plates and spoons that she washed in the kitchen to the number of steps she walked down a road. Mathematics came so naturally to Johnson that she skipped years of school!

Parameter path

Functions are helpful if you have to do the same thing many times in different places. However, what if you want to do something similar but not exactly the same? That's where parameters come in! Here, they'll help you solve a maze.

What are parameters?

Parameters are extra bits of information you can pass into a function when you want to customize how the function works. For example, you may make a function for a sprite to turn to the right and walk in that direction, but a parameter will let you change how far you want it to go.

moveRight(parameter)

1 Grab a piece of paper and a pencil, then take a look at the algorithm on the right. The blocks will tell you which direction you need to go to solve the maze, but not how far you have to move in each direction. See if you can write down the number of squares, or parameters, for each step to reach the cross.

Start here.

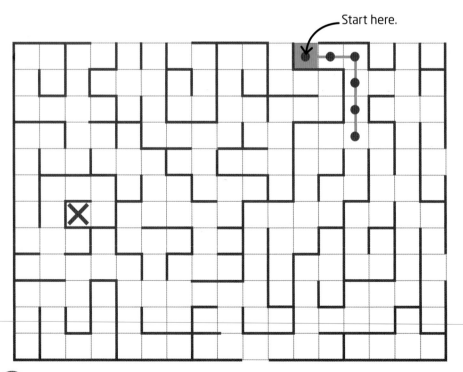

The first two steps have been done for you.

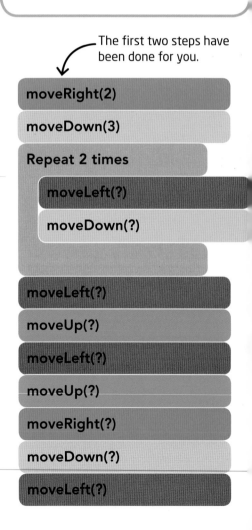

moveRight(2)

moveDown(3)

Repeat 2 times

    moveLeft(?)

    moveDown(?)

moveLeft(?)

moveUp(?)

moveLeft(?)

moveUp(?)

moveRight(?)

moveDown(?)

moveLeft(?)

Now try completing the algorithm below to solve this trickier maze. The same directions always use the same colored block. You can check your answers on page 135.

②

moveDown(?)

moveLeft(?)

moveDown(?)

moveRight(?)

Repeat ? times

> moveDown(?)

> moveRight(?)

moveDown(?)

moveRight(?)

moveUp(?)

Don't forget that a loop block will let you repeat more than one instruction several times in a row!

Now try...

Imagine moving the cross to a new position in the maze and then writing new instructions to get to it.

Decompose
a castle

You might have heard the word "decomposition" when talking about how food or leaves break down into compost. In computer science, instead of breaking down food, coders decompose problems into smaller pieces that are easier to solve. Can you decompose this castle to figure out how to make it?

1

Take a good look at this cardboard castle. Try to figure out how many different parts the castle is made up of and how each part is made.

Try and figure out the smallest pieces of each of the parts.

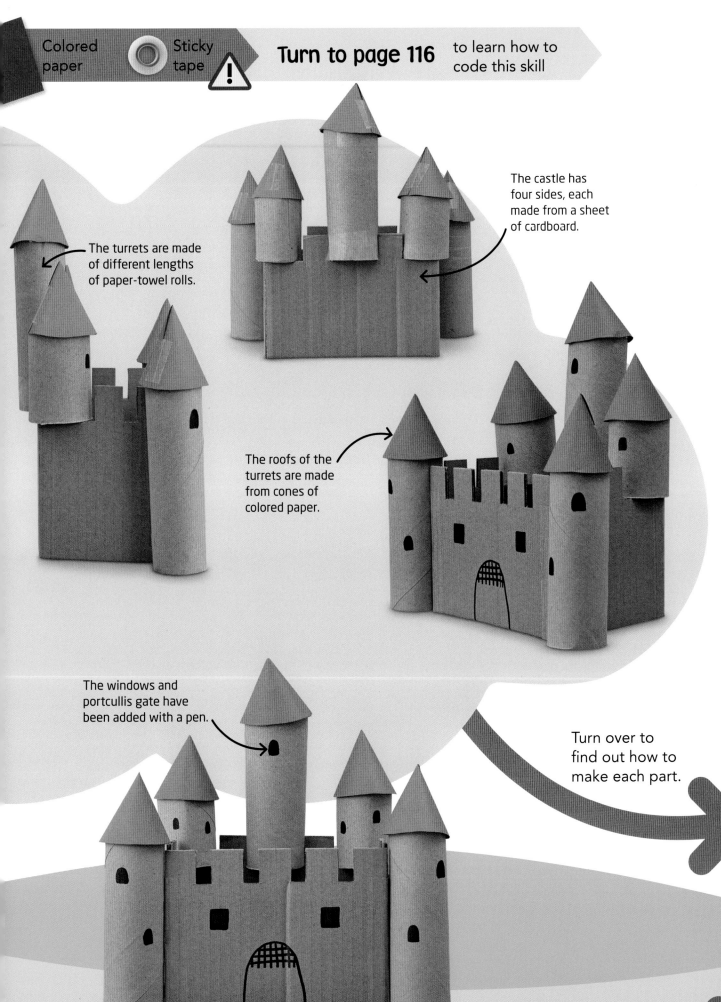

The turrets are made of different lengths of paper-towel rolls.

The castle has four sides, each made from a sheet of cardboard.

The roofs of the turrets are made from cones of colored paper.

The windows and portcullis gate have been added with a pen.

Turn over to find out how to make each part.

59

3 ⚠ To make your turrets, use a few tubes from the inside of a roll of paper towels and cut them to different heights.

2 ⚠ To make the castle walls, cut four rectangles of cardboard—two should be a bit longer for the front and back.

Cut out a few squares from the top of the wall to make toothed battlements.

The shorter pieces will be the sides of your castle.

Add some windows and a portcullis gate to the front piece.

Add windows to
the turrets using a
black felt-tip pen.

4 To make the turret
roofs, you need to
use safety scissors to
cut circles of colored
paper about an inch
wider than your
cardboard tubes.

Cut a straight
line to the
center of
the circle.

Fold one edge
under the other to
make a cone, then
tape it together.

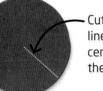

5

The castle looks complicated, but it is
actually only made of three similar parts!
Can you figure out how to fit all the
pieces together to make the castle?

Scorpion

Whip spider

Spider

Tick

1

Although they look different, all these animals are arachnids. Let's find a pattern. Can you write down at least three things they all have in common?

Which of these things do they have in common?

Eight legs

Wings

A head and body

Scaly skin

A hard outer skeleton

Pattern matching
creepy-crawlies

The ability to find and match patterns is what helps a programmer figure out how new problems might be similar to challenges that they've already solved. In this activity, we'll work to find some patterns in nature, and then see if those patterns can help us solve a new problem.

Centipede

Dragonfly

Bee

Mosquito

Beetle

②

These animals are all insects. What pattern of features can you see among them? Can you write down three things they have in common?

Which of these things do they have in common?

Two antennae

A furry tail

Wings

Six legs

A long neck

③

Using the patterns you found above, can you figure out which group each of these critters would belong to?

Earwig

→ Now try...

Write these patterns down and, with an adult, take your guide outside to find some real critters. Do they fit any of the patterns for creature types that you've already identified? Remember not to touch them!

Ant

Abstraction story

Abstraction is looking at the big picture, rather than all of the little details. When coding, programmers will often use abstraction to make a basic program that can be reused. They then add the details in later. You can use abstraction to write a story to match a set of pictures.

Some things only appear once or twice in the whole strip.

1

Look at the four pictures in each of the comic strips. There are several things that are the same and several things that are different in each strip.

Some things are in every frame in the strip.

Try writing your own story for this comic strip.

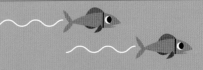

Turn to page 122 to learn how to code this skill

Important to the story	**Not important to the story**
Underwater	Fish
An octopus	Bubbles
A shark	Submarine
A treasure chest	Starfish
	Seaweed

2

Grab a notebook and make a list of at least four things that are in all four pictures. Those will become the important parts in your story. We've done this for the underwater images, and you can do it for the space images.

3

Make a list of at least four things that change. Those things shouldn't be in your story at all.

4

When you're done, use your important items to write a short story. Try to make sure that your story is written in such a way that it makes sense no matter which picture in the strip is selected to go with it.

One day Olly the octopus was swimming along underwater. He spotted an old, wooden chest and wanted to see what was inside. However, he couldn't open it. His friend Susie the shark used her teeth to pull it open. Inside, they found lots of treasure!

Once upon a time, I had a horse. He loved to run around the field. His favorite food was carrots and I talked to him every day.

Remixing rhymes

Remixing is a great way to learn how to code. You might find a program that does something amazing, however, it's much more fun to change, or "remix," it until it does exactly what you want. You can remix your favorite poems and stories, too!

1 Find a poem or short story that you like. If you want a challenge, pick a poem that rhymes.

<u>Playing sports</u> is really fun,
To <u>throw a ball, or jump, or run</u>.
There is nothing quite so <u>loud,</u>
As <u>the cheering of a crowd</u>.

<u>Painting portraits</u> is really fun,
To <u>color flowers</u>, <u>grass</u>, <u>and sun</u>.
There is nothing quite so <u>smart,</u>
As <u>a wall covered in art</u>.

2 Grab a notepad and rewrite the poem or story to be more personal to you. Try to replace at least one word in each line. Then read your remixed creation to a friend!

You might have to think hard to find a new rhyme when you remix a poem.

urn to page 126 to learn how to code this skill

i

Useful tip

Try and identify words that will be easy to change. Nouns, such as "horse" or "carrots," can be swapped easily. So can verbs like "playing" and "talked."

Nouns
Horse
Field
Carrots

Verbs
Playing
Throw
Talked

Once upon a time, I had a <u>horse</u>. He loved to run around the <u>field</u>. His favorite food was <u>carrots</u> and I <u>talked to</u> him every day.

↓

Once upon a time, I had a <u>cat</u>. He loved to run around the <u>room</u>. His favorite food was <u>fish</u> and I <u>brushed</u> him every day.

Why not make the poem or story more personal to you? You could make it about a pet or something you like to do.

Now try...

You can remix one of your favorite songs. Swap out the details to make it all about you!

The internet

The internet is a network of channels that connects your computer with other computers all over the world. If, for example, you send a message from your smartphone to a laptop, it has to travel through many different places in a very short amount of time to get there.

Core router

Core routers are at the heart of the internet. These huge machines are capable of directing and sending large amounts of information at very high speeds around the world.

Core router

Underwater cables carry data across the world. These cables are only about 1 in (2.5 cm) thick, but they carry huge amounts of data.

Undersea cables

Smartphone

Mobile tower

Telephone exchange

Internet Service Provider

Core router

Mobile connection

If you're connecting to the internet using a smartphone, then your data will be broadcast to a mobile tower using wireless radio waves. This tower sends the information through data lines in the ground to a telephone exchange.

Internet Service Provider

Also called an ISP, this is a company that connects you to the internet. Every device on the internet has a special code called an IP address that lets the ISP know where to send your data.

Telephone exchange

A connection is made between an ISP and the telephone lines by a telephone exchange. They connect the right person to their chosen ISP. Alternatively, an ISP connects to a home router directly by fiber-optic cables.

Home router

A home router is the piece of equipment that manages the transfer of information into, out of, and within your home. It makes sure that each device gets the data that it needs.

Internet Service Provider — Telephone exchange — Telephone lines — Home router — Wi-Fi — Laptop

Wires and cables

The information that you send through the internet might travel in different forms inside your home. However, once it leaves the building, it's probably being carried either by copper wires or fiber-optic cables made of glass.

Wi-Fi

Often called a "wireless" connection, Wi-Fi allows you to connect to the internet without being attached to any cables. Instead, your information is sent through the air using radio waves, between the router and your device.

Tim Berners-Lee

In 1989, British computer scientist Tim Berners-Lee invented the World Wide Web. Before Berners-Lee created this way of accessing information on the internet, each individual network had its own way of working. This meant that some areas could not talk to each other. Now, every part of the internet uses the same system, connecting people all over the world.

Inventor of the web, Tim Berners-Lee is the director of the World Wide Web Consortium, a group that makes sure the internet works well.

Debugging

Loops

Collisions

Decomposition

Algorithm

Events

Remixing

Pattern matching

Computer coding

Using code, you can create games, apps, and other programs that can help you with anything from escaping boredom to landing a rover on Mars! This chapter will show you how to start designing programs on a computer.

Getting Scratch

Scratch is a coding language that has been designed to be simple to use. It uses color-coded blocks to let you create programs and games easily. You can either use the Scratch website to create code or you can download it onto your computer so you can use it offline.

Get started

To get started, visit the Scratch website at:
http://scratch.mit.edu

You can use Scratch right away by clicking "Start Creating," but if you want to save or share your projects you need to create a Scratch account using an email address. To do this, click "Join" and pick a username and password. Always ask permission from an adult before you create an account and don't use your real name as your username—pick a code name!

ONLINE Go to the website and click "Start Creating" to make your project online.	There's no setup needed when playing with Scratch 3.0 online, unless you want to be able to save projects for later. If you do, you need to create an account.	Click "Start Creating" to begin. You will automatically be taken to the Scratch 3.0 platform, where you can begin working on your project.
① Setup		**② Launching Scratch**
OFFLINE Download Scratch 3.0 from http://scratch.mit. edu/download	Download the Scratch 3.0 installer, then double-click on it to open the downloaded file. Follow the instructions to install Scratch 3.0 onto your machine.	Find the place where you installed Scratch 3.0 on your computer and double-click the icon to launch the program.

Be safe online

When you share a project in Scratch, it is shared with everyone! This means that even people that you don't know can see your program, and even look inside of it. To keep yourself as safe as possible, make sure to follow these important tips.

Take care!

✓ **DO** Give yourself a code name.

✗ **DON'T** Use your real name or share any personal information online, such as where you live.

✓ **DO** Ask an adult to look at your project before you share it online.

✗ **DON'T** Add any personal information into your programs, or pictures of yourself.

✓ **DO** Respect other people online.

✗ **DON'T** Use or share an image without permission from the person who created it.

Different versions of Scratch

This book uses Scratch 3.0, the latest version of Scratch. If you only have Scratch 2.0, you can either go to the Scratch website and download the newer version or you can play with Scratch 3.0 online.

Scratch 2.0
The older version of Scratch has a slightly different layout.

Scratch 3.0
The latest version of Scratch should work on most computers and tablets.

If you have an account, the Scratch editor usually saves your work automatically, but if you want to be sure it's been saved, click on "Save now" in the upper-right-hand corner.

You can edit projects in the online version of Scratch 3.0 on most modern browsers (except for Internet Explorer) on most computers or tablets. It does not currently work on phones.

③ Saving work

To save your work on the desktop version, go to the "File" menu and click "Save to your computer" from the dropdown.

④ Operating systems

The desktop version of Scratch 3.0 is available for PCs operating Windows 10 or newer, and Apple computers running MacOS 10.13 or newer.

Coding in Scratch

The blocks in Scratch are color-coded according to what sort of code they run. Snapping them together is as easy as drag, drop, click! Here are some tips and tricks that will have you building and running exciting programs in no time.

Types of block

There are nine main types of block in Scratch. Each block type has a special color so that you know where to find it in the Blocks Palette and what type of code it runs.

My super senses tell me this is an event!

Motion
Blocks that make your sprite move, turn, glide, or point in one direction are blue, and found in the Motion section.

Looks
Purple Looks blocks affect the way a sprite appears. This includes adding speech bubbles and costume changes.

Sound
Sound effects and volume blocks are pink and listed as part of the Sound category.

Events
Event blocks are yellow and have a domed top. They start code running.

Control
Loops, stops, pauses, and clones are all Control blocks, and they are orange.

Sensing
Sensing blocks are blocks that check what your sprites are doing. They are turquoise and pointed at the ends.

Operators
Green Operator blocks perform operations such as calculations, or combine Sensing blocks.

Variables
Variables are dark orange. You can create Variables according to what you need.

You can add extensions to the Blocks Palette by clicking here. Extension blocks are all the same color, but allow you to add music, video, and other features to your program.

Select **Music** to add music to your code.

Click on **Pen** to be able to make your sprite draw.

Select **Video Sensing** to use your webcam.

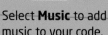

My Blocks
You can create your own blocks, called functions, and they are a reddish pink.

Flow of scripts

Each stack of blocks is called a script. Scripts run in order, from top to bottom. Different scripts can run at the same time, but each instruction in a particular script will run immediately after the instruction before it is finished.

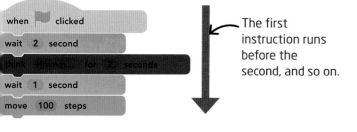

The first instruction runs before the second, and so on.

Running scripts

To run your script, click on it in the Scripts Area or do what is shown on the event at the very top. If you want to run two lines of code at the same time, you can build two different programs with the same event on top.

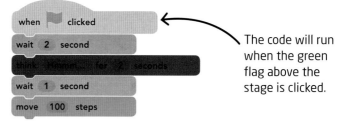

The code will run when the green flag above the stage is clicked.

Pixels in Scratch

Pixels are used to make up images on a screen, but in Scratch they are also used as locations that tell the computer where to put something.

The entire Scratch stage is divided into an area that is 480 pixels wide and 360 pixels tall.

go to x: 0 y: 0

The Scratch stage is divided into square pixels. Under the Motion category, you'll see blocks that have a spot for both x and y locations. If you want to move a sprite across by one pixel, you put "go to x:1." If you want to move a sprite up by one pixel, you put "go to y:1." Negative values move your sprite left or down. The center of the stage is where x is 0 and y is 0.

go to x: -100 y: 0

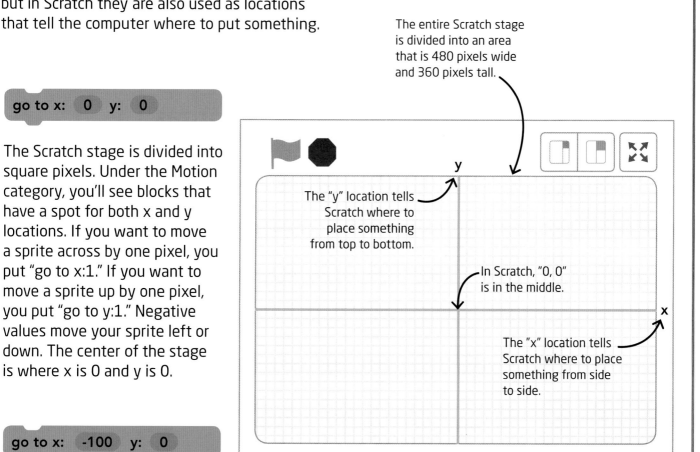

The "y" location tells Scratch where to place something from top to bottom.

In Scratch, "0, 0" is in the middle.

The "x" location tells Scratch where to place something from side to side.

Algorithms

An algorithm is a list of steps that tells you how to do something. When professional coders start programming, they like to have a clear algorithm so that they know what to make. In this activity, you'll make your own algorithm and prepare for building your first program.

Getting the order right

You might know what you want a program to do, but if you put the steps in the wrong order, it won't work. Take a look at this example to see how the sequence can be important to an algorithm. What order would we put these instructions in if we want our cat to walk, turn around, come back, then tell us that it's tired?

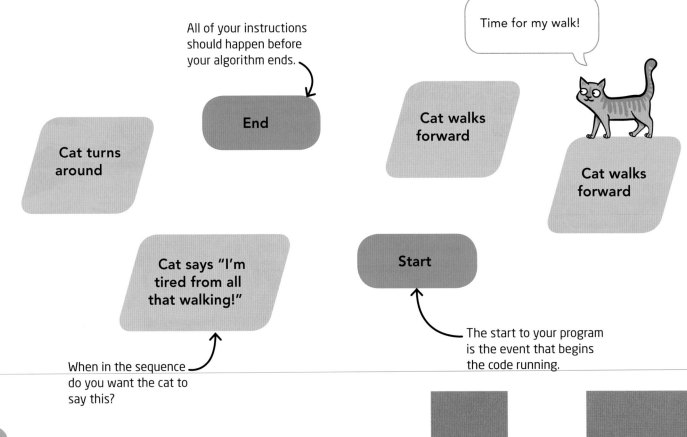

All of your instructions should happen before your algorithm ends.

Time for my walk!

End

Cat walks forward

Cat turns around

Cat walks forward

Cat says "I'm tired from all that walking!"

Start

When in the sequence do you want the cat to say this?

The start to your program is the event that begins the code running.

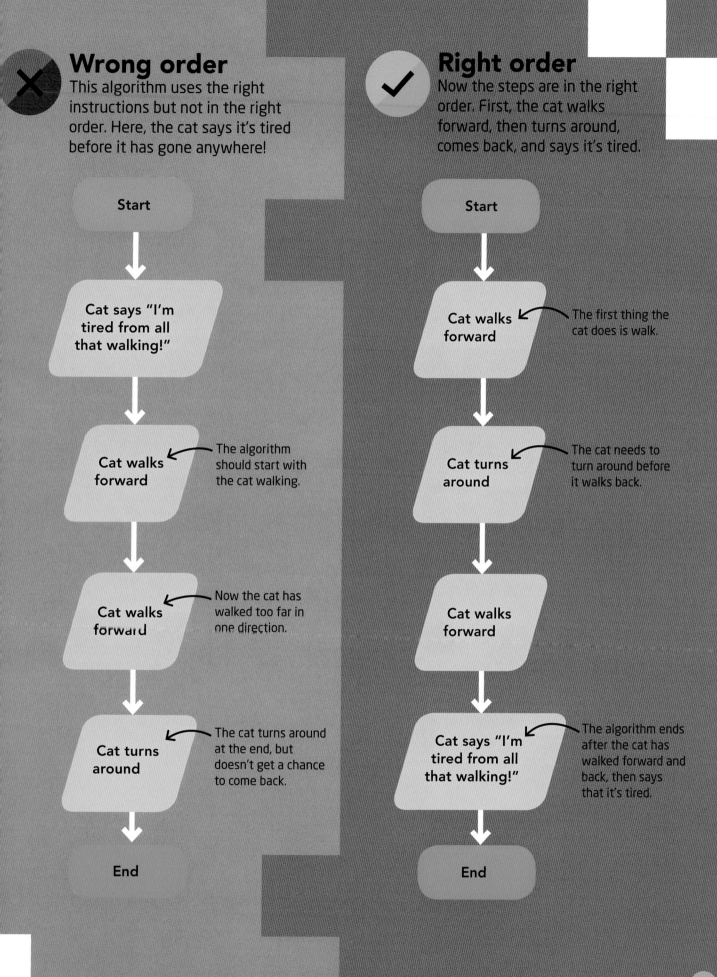

✕ Wrong order

This algorithm uses the right instructions but not in the right order. Here, the cat says it's tired before it has gone anywhere!

Start

Cat says "I'm tired from all that walking!"

Cat walks forward
— The algorithm should start with the cat walking.

Cat walks forward
— Now the cat has walked too far in one direction.

Cat turns around
— The cat turns around at the end, but doesn't get a chance to come back.

End

✓ Right order

Now the steps are in the right order. First, the cat walks forward, then turns around, comes back, and says it's tired.

Start

Cat walks forward
— The first thing the cat does is walk.

Cat turns around
— The cat needs to turn around before it walks back.

Cat walks forward

Cat says "I'm tired from all that walking!"
— The algorithm ends after the cat has walked forward and back, then says that it's tired.

End

Adding detail

When an algorithm is too simple, it can miss important details. This can lead to a misunderstanding when it's time to code. In order to avoid issues later, it's helpful to add as much detail to your algorithm as you can think of so the computer does exactly what you expect when it reads your code.

To turn around, the cat needs to flip from left to right. If it simply turned around it would be upside down.

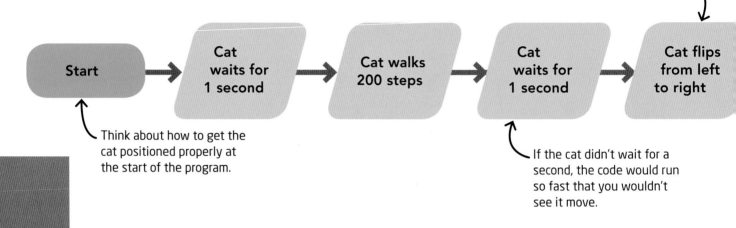

Think about how to get the cat positioned properly at the start of the program.

If the cat didn't wait for a second, the code would run so fast that you wouldn't see it move.

The program

Once you have planned out your algorithm, you need to find the right blocks to make it happen.

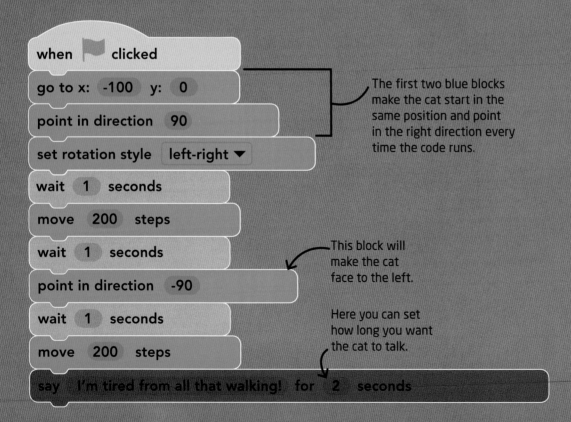

The first two blue blocks make the cat start in the same position and point in the right direction every time the code runs.

This block will make the cat face to the left.

Here you can set how long you want the cat to talk.

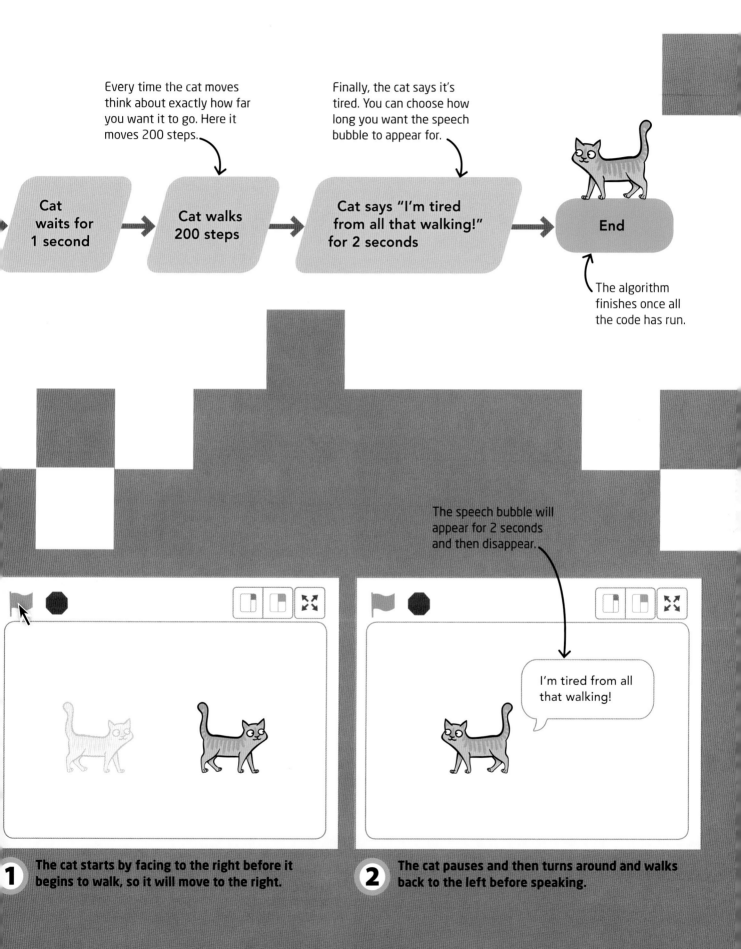

Every time the cat moves think about exactly how far you want it to go. Here it moves 200 steps.

Finally, the cat says it's tired. You can choose how long you want the speech bubble to appear for.

Cat waits for 1 second

Cat walks 200 steps

Cat says "I'm tired from all that walking!" for 2 seconds

End

The algorithm finishes once all the code has run.

The speech bubble will appear for 2 seconds and then disappear.

I'm tired from all that walking!

1 The cat starts by facing to the right before it begins to walk, so it will move to the right.

2 The cat pauses and then turns around and walks back to the left before speaking.

Scratch

Date created: 2003
Creator: Massachusetts Institute of Technology (MIT)
Country: USA
Text or blocks: Blocks

Scratch is a visual programming language. Code is written by dragging blocks from a special toolbox. This is great for new coders, since commands are premade and easy to use, but advanced users might prefer a text language where they have more freedom.

when 🚩 clicked

say   Hello, World!

Type your phrase into the "say" block and Scratch will have your character say it!

Python

Date created: 1991
Creator: Guido van Rossum
Country: The Netherlands
Text or blocks: Text

Python is a text-based language. It's a great tool for teaching people to code, since it stresses good habits. However, Python could not be used for programming 3-D games or other tasks that require a lot of computer memory.

print("Hello, World!")

In Python, you must tell the program to print your command, then it will show up on-screen.

Programming languages

Programming languages, or computer languages, are sets of code that computers can understand. Each language has its good points and bad points. Depending on what a programmer needs, they might find that a certain language works better than another for what they want to do.

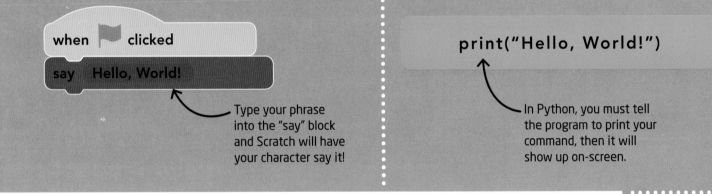

JavaScript

Date created: 1995
Creator: Brendan Eich
Country: USA
Text or blocks: Text

JavaScript is everywhere! It's very fast and used by lots of applications, especially web pages! However, it runs on the user's computer—not on an online server—so it can be less secure than other languages, and can look different, depending on the browser you use.

```
alert ("Hello, World !") ;
```

This command will get JavaScript to show your phrase in a pop-up box in your browser.

Ruby

Date created: 1995
Creator: Yukihiro Matsumoto
Country: Japan
Text or blocks: Text

Ruby is a fairly simple language that allows a lot of freedom and flexibility. It is very popular and great for beginners, but because it doesn't require a strict structure, bugs can be introduced in Ruby that are well disguised and very hard to find!

```
puts "Hello, World!"
```

This command is just like "print" in Python. It tells Ruby to show your phrase on-screen.

"Hello, World!"

It's a tradition among programmers to have the first program say the phrase "Hello, World!" when testing the new language. Some coders believe that they can tell how difficult a language will be based on how easily they can get the computer to say "Hello, World!" in that language.

C++

Date created: 1969
Creator: Bjarne Stroustrup
Country: USA
Text or blocks: Text

C++ is a complex language that is very popular with professionals because of its speed and reliability. However, it's not always the best language for new programmers, since it requires a lot of code to do even simple tasks.

```
#include <stdio.h>
main{}{printf("Hello, World!";}
```

Coding programs

You have already learned that an algorithm is a list of steps that tells you to do something. Programming is "translating" that algorithm into code. A clear algorithm will help you prepare for writing your first program.

(1) Plan

The first step to making your program is to figure out what you want to do. In this program, we want to make a pirate say "Ahoy!," walk across the stage, then stop and say "Let's walk, matey," before walking off the screen

This tells us where our program starts. If it's easier, you can stack your instructions from top to bottom instead of left to right.

Start

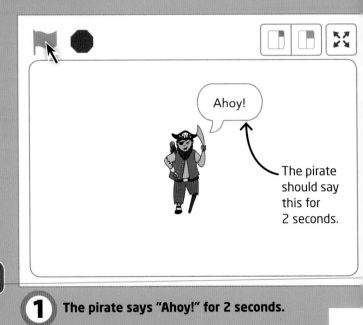

(3) Putting it in Scratch

Once you have created your algorithm, all you have to do is work out which block makes each step happen and add it to your code!

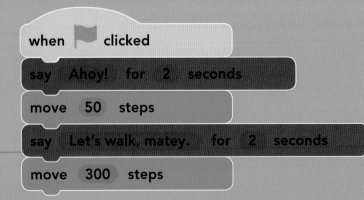

```
when ⚑ clicked
say  Ahoy!  for  2  seconds
move  50  steps
say  Let's walk, matey.  for  2  seconds
move  300  steps
```

Ahoy!

The pirate should say this for 2 seconds.

(1) The pirate says "Ahoy!" for 2 seconds.

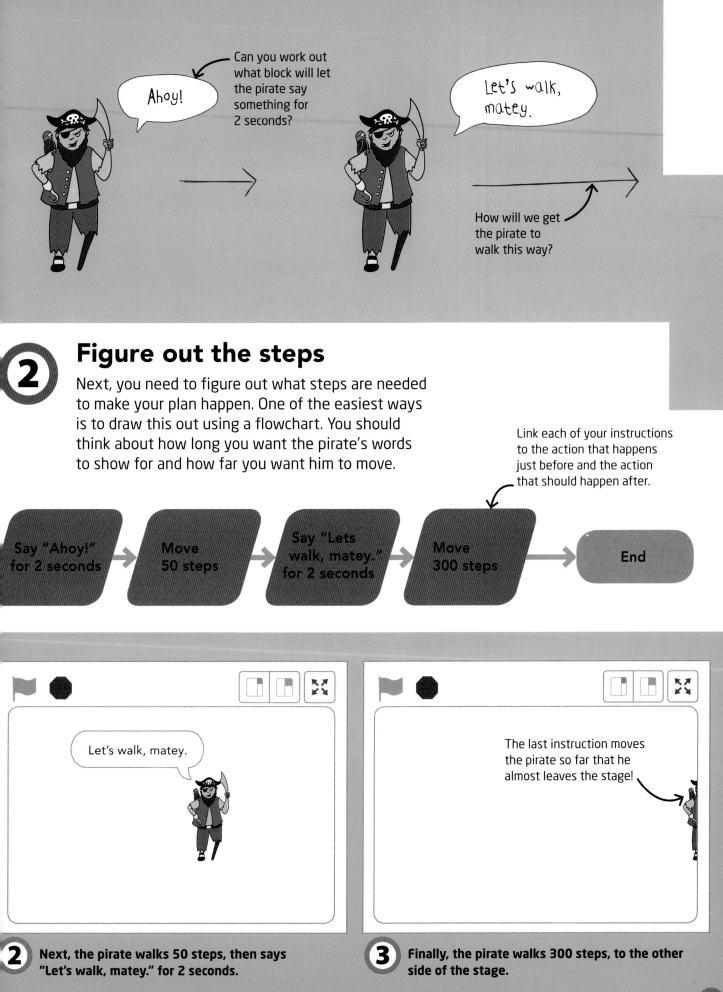

Can you work out what block will let the pirate say something for 2 seconds?

Ahoy!

Let's walk, matey.

How will we get the pirate to walk this way?

2 Figure out the steps

Next, you need to figure out what steps are needed to make your plan happen. One of the easiest ways is to draw this out using a flowchart. You should think about how long you want the pirate's words to show for and how far you want him to move.

Link each of your instructions to the action that happens just before and the action that should happen after.

Say "Ahoy!" for 2 seconds → Move 50 steps → Say "Lets walk, matey." for 2 seconds → Move 300 steps → End

Let's walk, matey.

The last instruction moves the pirate so far that he almost leaves the stage!

2 Next, the pirate walks 50 steps, then says "Let's walk, matey." for 2 seconds.

3 Finally, the pirate walks 300 steps, to the other side of the stage.

Debugging

Sometimes we know exactly what we want an algorithm to do but our program just doesn't work. When that happens, it doesn't usually make sense to throw all of the code out and start over. Instead, you can look for errors, also called bugs, that you can fix.

What the program should do

This program will first move the sprite to the other side of the stage. Then the sprite pauses before hiding and reappearing in a completely new position.

The program

Try coding the blocks in step 1 and running it in Scratch. There are a few bugs in this program. Can you work through the steps below to make the program do what it is supposed to do? Look at the next step to help you.

1 The sprite spins around here, which we don't want it to do. One of the blocks is incorrect and needs to be changed.

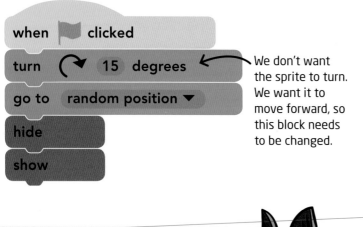

We don't want the sprite to turn. We want it to move forward, so this block needs to be changed.

2 The program moves so fast that you can't see the sprite move at the beginning. Wait blocks need to be added to slow the sprite down.

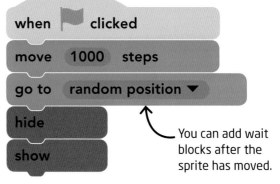

You can add wait blocks after the sprite has moved.

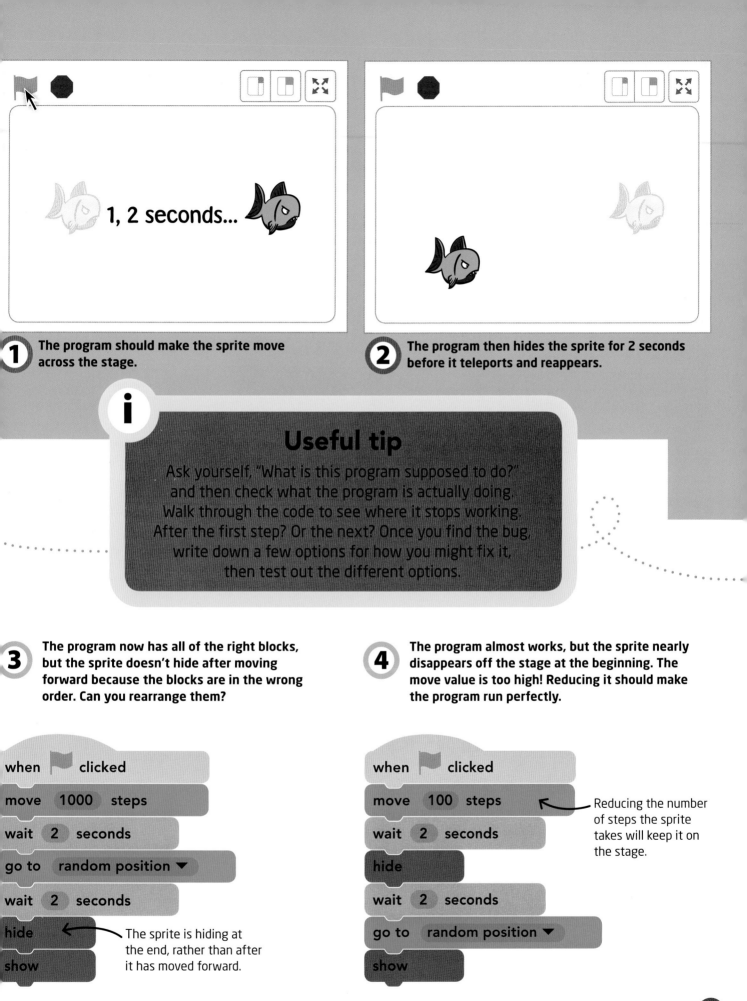

1 The program should make the sprite move across the stage.

2 The program then hides the sprite for 2 seconds before it teleports and reappears.

Useful tip

Ask yourself, "What is this program supposed to do?" and then check what the program is actually doing. Walk through the code to see where it stops working. After the first step? Or the next? Once you find the bug, write down a few options for how you might fix it, then test out the different options.

3 The program now has all of the right blocks, but the sprite doesn't hide after moving forward because the blocks are in the wrong order. Can you rearrange them?

4 The program almost works, but the sprite nearly disappears off the stage at the beginning. The move value is too high! Reducing it should make the program run perfectly.

when [flag] clicked
move 1000 steps
wait 2 seconds
go to random position ▼
wait 2 seconds
hide
show

The sprite is hiding at the end, rather than after it has moved forward.

when [flag] clicked
move 100 steps
wait 2 seconds
hide
wait 2 seconds
go to random position ▼
show

Reducing the number of steps the sprite takes will keep it on the stage.

Why use loops?

It can be very useful to make a program that does something over and over. Loops let you create sprites that keep changing color or never stop moving. A forever loop is great for this. The only way to stop this type of loop from running is to stop the whole program.

1 Here, we want an octopus sprite to keep changing color every second. Without a loop, you have to add two new blocks for every color change.

2 By placing the color change blocks inside a forever loop, the octopus will go on changing color forever, without you having to add any extra code.

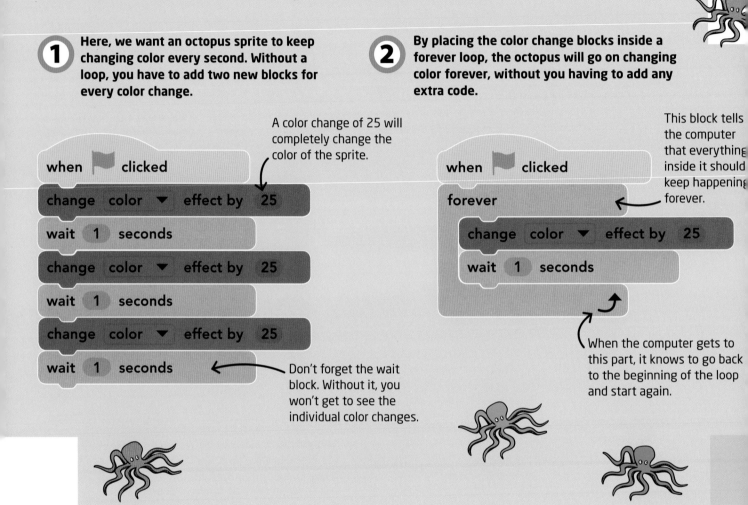

A color change of 25 will completely change the color of the sprite.

when ⚑ clicked
change color ▼ effect by 25
wait 1 seconds
change color ▼ effect by 25
wait 1 seconds
change color ▼ effect by 25
wait 1 seconds

Don't forget the wait block. Without it, you won't get to see the individual color changes.

This block tells the computer that everything inside it should keep happening forever.

when ⚑ clicked
forever
change color ▼ effect by 25
wait 1 seconds

When the computer gets to this part, it knows to go back to the beginning of the loop and start again.

Loops

Programs become much more powerful once you start adding loops. A loop block repeats everything inside it so you don't have to create the same code again and again. One simple loop can help your program do so much more.

Breaking loops

Not all loops go on forever. You can also use loops that stop after they repeat a certain number of times, or loops that will stop when you do something special. This is useful when you want something to keep changing until an event happens.

Useful tip

There are 199 different color effects that every sprite can be in Scratch. A change of 25 will completely change the color; a change of 1 will change it only slightly. Remember, changing the color effect will shift all of the colors of the sprite.

1 A repeat loop with a changeable value lets you choose how many times you want the code inside the block to repeat. If you want this monster sprite to change color three times, you simply put 3 in the loop.

```
when [flag] clicked
repeat 3
    change color ▼ effect by 25
    wait 1 seconds
```

This loop looks a lot like the first one, but it will stop after the color has changed 3 times.

The colors of the sprites will change by the same amount each time, but the number of times the color changes depends on the loop you use.

2 If you want a loop to keep repeating until an event happens, you can use a repeat until loop. Here, the monster sprite will keep changing color until the space bar is pressed.

```
when [flag] clicked
repeat until < key space▼ pressed? >
    change color ▼ effect by 25
    wait 1 seconds
```

The loop will stop when this condition of the space bar being pressed is true.

Now try...

What happens when you put a repeat loop inside another repeat loop? Play with it and see! Can you make a sprite keep jumping to new positions but have it change color a few times before it jumps again?

```
repeat 10
    repeat 4
```

91

The program

The program below turns this unicorn sprite into a pen! Build the code below and see what you can create. Can you draw a square?

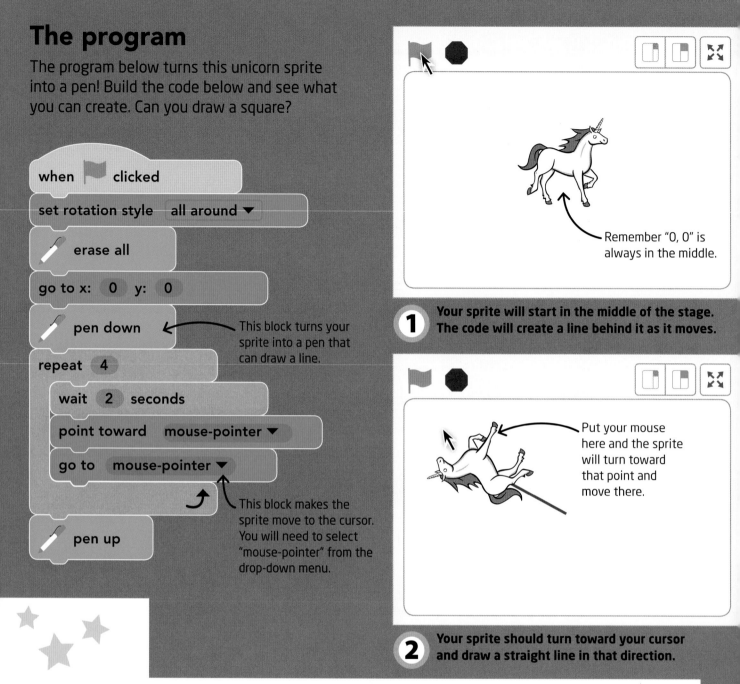

```
when 🚩 clicked
set rotation style  all around ▼
🖊 erase all
go to x: 0  y: 0
🖊 pen down
repeat 4
    wait 2 seconds
    point toward  mouse-pointer ▼
    go to  mouse-pointer ▼
🖊 pen up
```

This block turns your sprite into a pen that can draw a line.

This block makes the sprite move to the cursor. You will need to select "mouse-pointer" from the drop-down menu.

Remember "0, 0" is always in the middle.

1 Your sprite will start in the middle of the stage. The code will create a line behind it as it moves.

Put your mouse here and the sprite will turn toward that point and move there.

2 Your sprite should turn toward your cursor and draw a straight line in that direction.

Creativity

Programming can be creative, artistic, and fun! All you have to do to make something special is keep trying different ideas until you figure out how to put it into code. Sometimes the most amazing projects are the ones that don't turn out as expected!

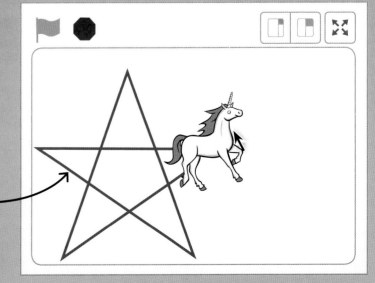

Useful tip

To remove all the lines drawn by a sprite, click on the "erase all" block in the Pen section of the Blocks Palette, or add it to your program.

You choose where the sprite goes each time the loop runs.

The given program lets you move the sprite four times.

3 Get creative and use your sprite to draw different shapes. How many shapes can you make with the program?

Now try...

Can you use your program to draw a hexagon? Can you change it so that you can? Now what else can you draw?

If you can change the program to let you draw a hexagon, you can draw a star as well.

Collaboration

Collaboration means working together, and it's a powerful tool! If you get stuck, then working with others can help you come up with ideas that you might not have thought of by yourself.

The program

Here are three scripts that will all play a rhythm on a different drum at the same time. Can you collaborate with these programs by adding a fourth drum?

1

Copy each of these three scripts, then click the green flag to listen to what they sound like together.

Bongos

when 🏳 clicked

repeat 8
- ♫ rest for 0.25 beats
- ♫ rest for 0.25 beats
- ♫ play drum (13) Bongo ▼ for 0.25 beats
- ♫ play drum (13) Bongo ▼ for 0.25 beats

These blocks play the drum for a set number of beats.

Scratch lets you choose from 18 different drums. This code uses bongos.

when 🏳 clicked

repeat 8
- ♫ play drum (1) Snare Drum ▼ for 0.25 beats
- ♫ play drum (1) Snare Drum ▼ for 0.25 beats
- ♫ rest for 0.25 beats
- ♫ rest for 0.25 beats

Snare drum

No sound will play during the rests. These sections will be silent while the other drums play.

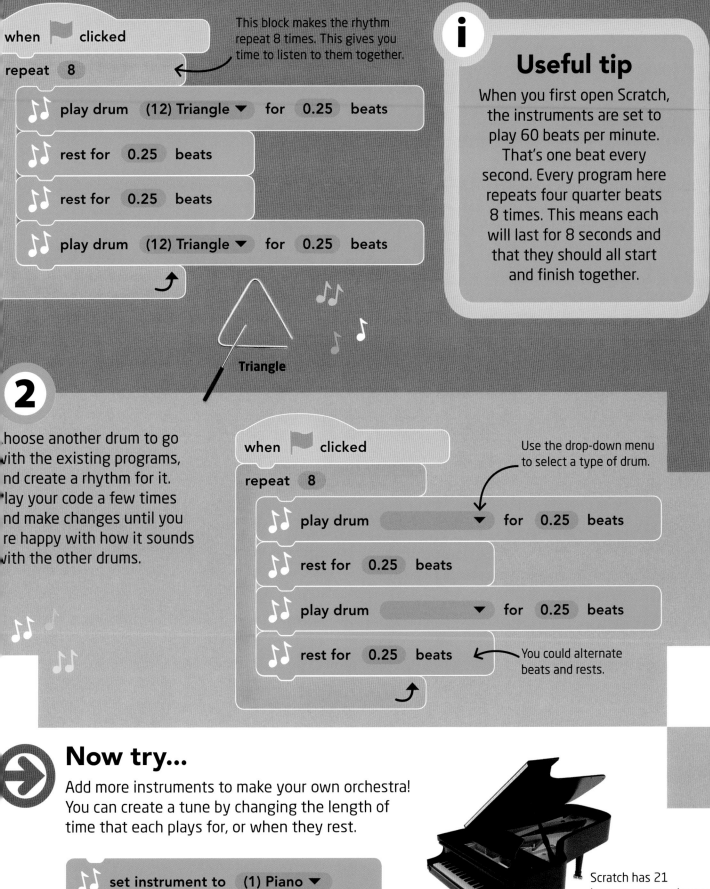

when ⚑ clicked

repeat 8

♫ play drum (12) Triangle ▼ for 0.25 beats

♫ rest for 0.25 beats

♫ rest for 0.25 beats

♫ play drum (12) Triangle ▼ for 0.25 beats

This block makes the rhythm repeat 8 times. This gives you time to listen to them together.

i

Useful tip

When you first open Scratch, the instruments are set to play 60 beats per minute. That's one beat every second. Every program here repeats four quarter beats 8 times. This means each will last for 8 seconds and that they should all start and finish together.

Triangle

2

Choose another drum to go with the existing programs, and create a rhythm for it. Play your code a few times and make changes until you're happy with how it sounds with the other drums.

when ⚑ clicked

repeat 8

♫ play drum ▼ for 0.25 beats

♫ rest for 0.25 beats

♫ play drum ▼ for 0.25 beats

♫ rest for 0.25 beats

Use the drop-down menu to select a type of drum.

You could alternate beats and rests.

Now try...

Add more instruments to make your own orchestra! You can create a tune by changing the length of time that each plays for, or when they rest.

♫ set instrument to (1) Piano ▼

♫ play note 60 for 0.25 beats

Scratch has 21 instruments to choose from on the "set instruments" block, including a piano.

Persistence

Programming can be confusing, and sometimes it's difficult. It's possible that your code won't always work perfectly the first time you run it. You might have to debug it several times before it does what you want it to, but that's okay. Just keep trying!

The program

This program can make different patterns using a sprite. However, each one is missing some code. Can you figure out how to make the sprite create the patterns shown?

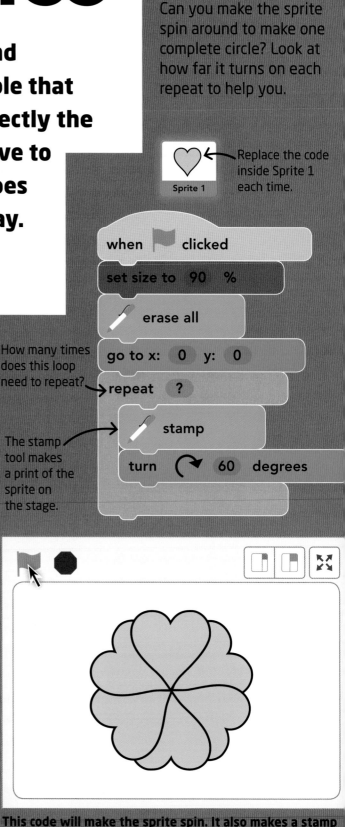

1

Can you make the sprite spin around to make one complete circle? Look at how far it turns on each repeat to help you.

Replace the code inside Sprite 1 each time.

Sprite 1

```
when [flag] clicked
set size to 90 %
erase all
go to x: 0 y: 0
repeat ?
    stamp
turn ↻ 60 degrees
```

How many times does this loop need to repeat?

The stamp tool makes a print of the sprite on the stage.

This code will make the sprite spin. It also makes a stamp of the sprite on the stage before it moves again.

To make the sprite spin from the bottom, you need to edit it in the Costumes editor.

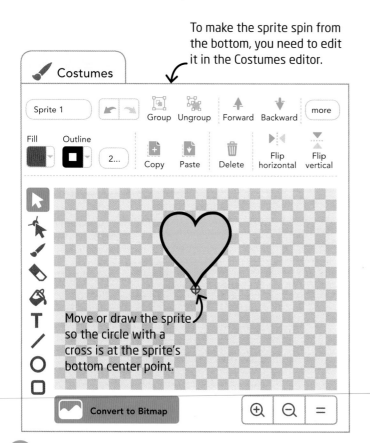

Move or draw the sprite so the circle with a cross is at the sprite's bottom center point.

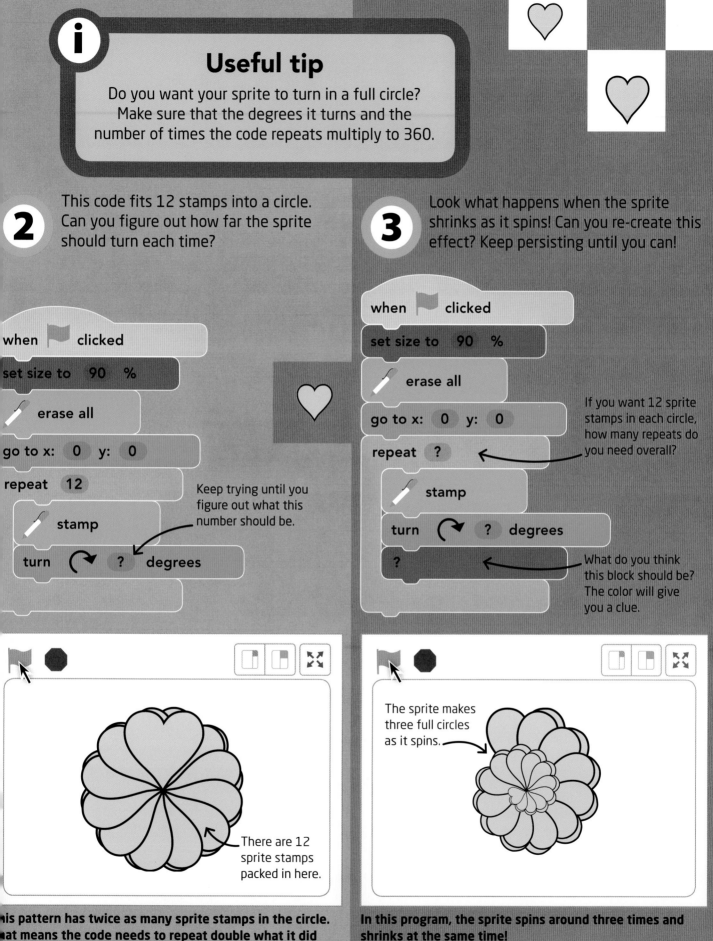

Useful tip

Do you want your sprite to turn in a full circle? Make sure that the degrees it turns and the number of times the code repeats multiply to 360.

2 This code fits 12 stamps into a circle. Can you figure out how far the sprite should turn each time?

3 Look what happens when the sprite shrinks as it spins! Can you re-create this effect? Keep persisting until you can!

when ⚑ clicked

set size to 90 %

🖌 erase all

go to x: 0 y: 0

repeat 12

  🖌 stamp

  turn ↻ ? degrees

Keep trying until you figure out what this number should be.

when ⚑ clicked

set size to 90 %

🖌 erase all

go to x: 0 y: 0

repeat ?

  🖌 stamp

  turn ↻ ? degrees

  ?

If you want 12 sprite stamps in each circle, how many repeats do you need overall?

What do you think this block should be? The color will give you a clue.

There are 12 sprite stamps packed in here.

The sprite makes three full circles as it spins.

This pattern has twice as many sprite stamps in the circle. That means the code needs to repeat double what it did before, but that the sprite should turn fewer degrees.

In this program, the sprite spins around three times and shrinks at the same time!

Conditionals

The programs that we've written so far have been fun, but they're about to get a whole lot better! Conditionals let the computer make decisions based on whether a condition is true or false, which lets you create programs that can change.

Types of conditional

These orange blocks are conditionals. You add a turquoise "condition" block to them so that the computer knows whether or not to run the code inside. If the condition is true, the computer will do one thing. If the condition is false, it will do something else, or nothing at all.

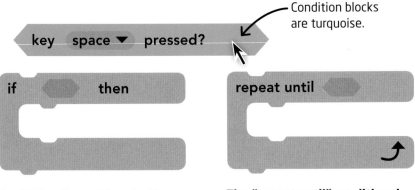

Condition blocks are turquoise.

key space ▼ pressed?

if ⬡ then

An "if then" conditional will only run the code inside it if the condition attached to it is true.

repeat until ⬡

The "repeat until" conditional will repeat code inside it until the condition attached to it is true.

What is a condition?

A condition is a statement that can either be true or false. For example, if you press the space bar on your keyboard, then the condition "key space pressed" is true. In Scratch, conditions are turquoise blocks with pointed ends.

A sprite can collide with another sprite or the edge of the stage.

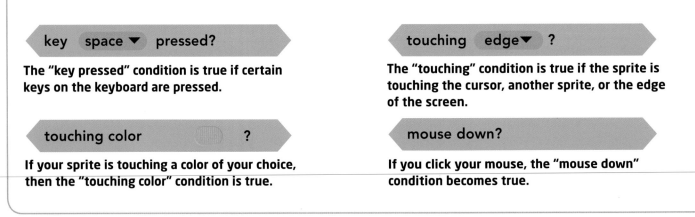

key space ▼ pressed?

The "key pressed" condition is true if certain keys on the keyboard are pressed.

touching color ⬡ ?

If your sprite is touching a color of your choice, then the "touching color" condition is true.

touching edge▼ ?

The "touching" condition is true if the sprite is touching the cursor, another sprite, or the edge of the screen.

mouse down?

If you click your mouse, the "mouse down" condition becomes true.

The program

This program challenges you to press the space bar when you think the crab is touching the edge of the stage. Take a good look and see if you can identify the conditionals and the conditions in the code.

This condition means the code in the conditional will keep running until the space bar is pressed.

```
when 🏴 clicked

go to x: 0 y: 0

repeat until  key space ▼ pressed?

    go to x: pick random -200 to 200   y: pick random -200 to 200

    wait 1 seconds

if  touching edge ▼ ?  then

    say You win! for 2 seconds
```

Each time the code runs, this block picks a random position for the sprite to appear in.

This condition asks whether the sprite is touching the edge of the stage, but the program will never get to it unless the space bar is pressed.

If the sprite is touching the edge, then the "touching edge?" condition is true and the sprite will say this. Otherwise, the program will end.

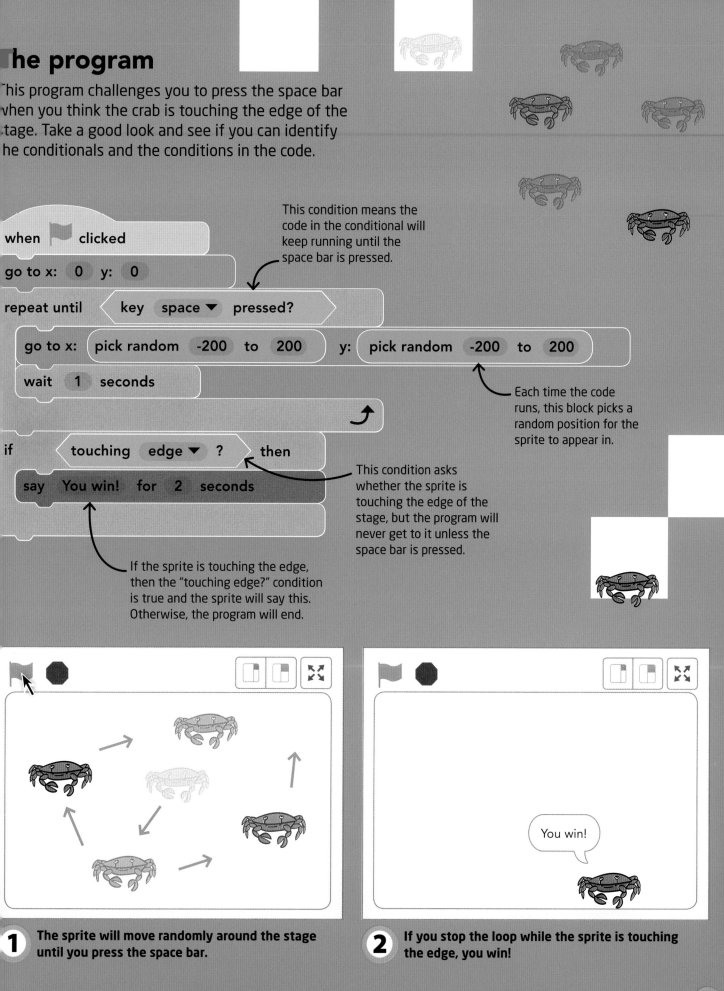

You win!

1 The sprite will move randomly around the stage until you press the space bar.

2 If you stop the loop while the sprite is touching the edge, you win!

99

If/else

It's great to be able to run a set of code if a condition is true, but it's even better to be able to run a different set of code if it's not! That's why we have if/else blocks. An if/else block is a type of conditional that will let you tell the computer what to do whether your condition is true or false.

The program

Here is some code that will make a sprite dance whenever you press the space bar, by flipping it from left to right. A "forever" loop makes the "if then else" block keep checking to see if the sprite should flip.

The "forever" loop around the "if then else" block makes the program keep checking whether the space bar is pressed.

The "if then else" block checks if the condition "key space pressed?" is true or false.

If the "if then else" block finds the "key space pressed?" condition true, the sprite will face to the left.

If the "if then else" block finds the "key space pressed?" condition false, the sprite will face to the right.

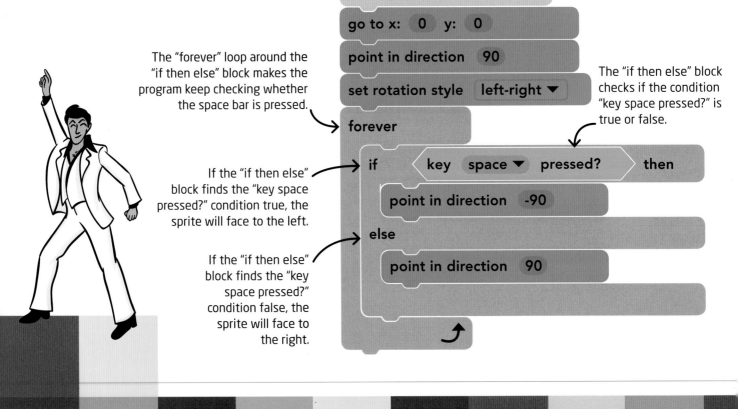

The "if then else" block

The "if then else" block is a conditional, but unlike the "if then" or "repeat until" conditionals, it holds two sets of code. This means you can ask the computer to do different things depending on if your condition is true or false.

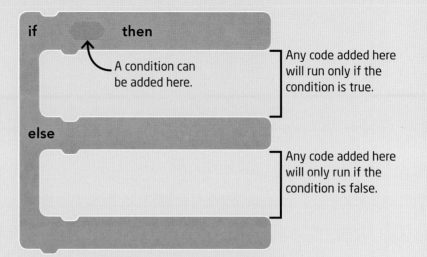

A condition can be added here.

Any code added here will run only if the condition is true.

Any code added here will only run if the condition is false.

i

Useful tip

Don't forget to add code to position your sprite properly at the beginning of each program. If you don't, you might have settings left over from previous code that makes the sprite do something that you didn't want.

1 Your sprite will start by facing to the right, but if you press the space bar it will flip to the left.

2 If the space bar isn't pressed, the sprite will stay facing the right. If you keep pressing and releasing the space bar, the sprite will dance on the spot.

Events

Up to this point, we've only started actions when the green flag is clicked. However, that is only one type of event used to trigger a piece of code. You can use different events to make a game more fun by starting actions while a program is already running.

Types of event

Event blocks make certain sections of code run when something special happens. For many programs, the code runs when the green flag is clicked, but code can also be run after a set amount of time, when you click on a sprite, when you press a certain key, or when another event happens.

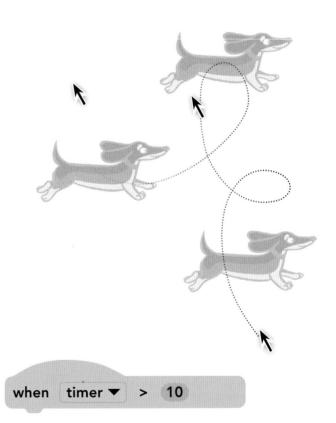

```
when ⚑ clicked
```

This block lets you start running the code connected to it by clicking the green flag on top of the stage.

```
when this sprite clicked
```

When you click on a certain sprite, this event block runs the code attached to it.

```
when timer ▼ > 10
```

When a timer gets above 10, or another value of your choice, the code connected to this block will run.

```
when space ▼ key pressed
```

The code connected to this block will run only when the space bar is pressed.

```
when backdrop switches to backdrop1 ▼
```

This block will run the connected code when the backdrop of your program is coded to change to a different picture.

This event block starts the dog running around the screen.

```
when ⚑ clicked
forever
    wait 0.5 seconds
    go to x: pick random -100 to 100  y: pick random -100 to 100
```

The dog will appear in random positions around the stage.

This event block will make the dog bark when you press the space bar.

```
when space ▼ key pressed
say Woof! for 2 seconds
```

This event block makes the dog say "You got me!" when you click on it.

```
when this sprite clicked
say You got me! for 2 seconds
go to x: 0 y: 0
stop all ▼
```

The program

You can use more than one event block in the same program to make different things happen. Here's the code for a game where you have to catch a running dog or make it bark. Can you figure out how to play?

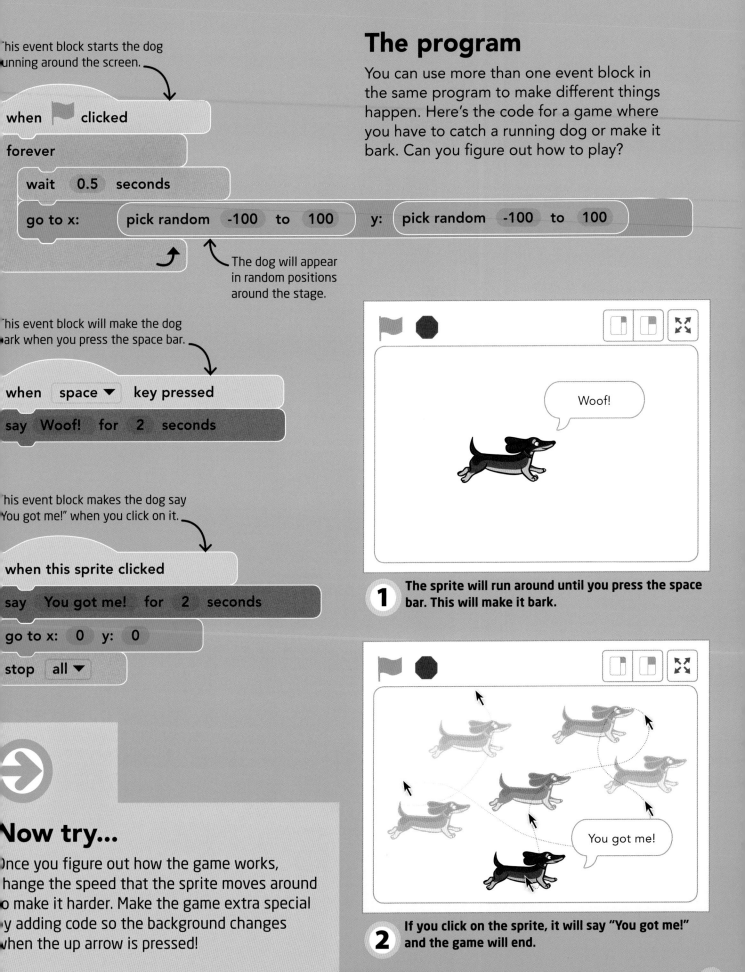

Woof!

1 The sprite will run around until you press the space bar. This will make it bark.

You got me!

2 If you click on the sprite, it will say "You got me!" and the game will end.

Now try...

Once you figure out how the game works, change the speed that the sprite moves around to make it harder. Make the game extra special by adding code so the background changes when the up arrow is pressed!

103

Input/ output

When you click on a sprite using your mouse, or press a key on your keyboard, you are providing your computer with input. These inputs affect the outputs from your screen or speakers. You can even use input from a webcam to make your programs interactive!

Permissions

This program requires the use of a webcam. Scratch needs your permission to use input from your webcam. When you click on the Video Sensing option, a pop-up window will ask you to allow or block it. You will only be able to try this program if you click allow.

Scratch.mit.edu wants to   x

📹 Use your camera

Block   Allow

The program

In this program, you try to catch Sprite 2 using Sprite 1, but you control the sprite by waving your arms around!

1 This script will make a sprite move around the screen until it touches the other sprite.

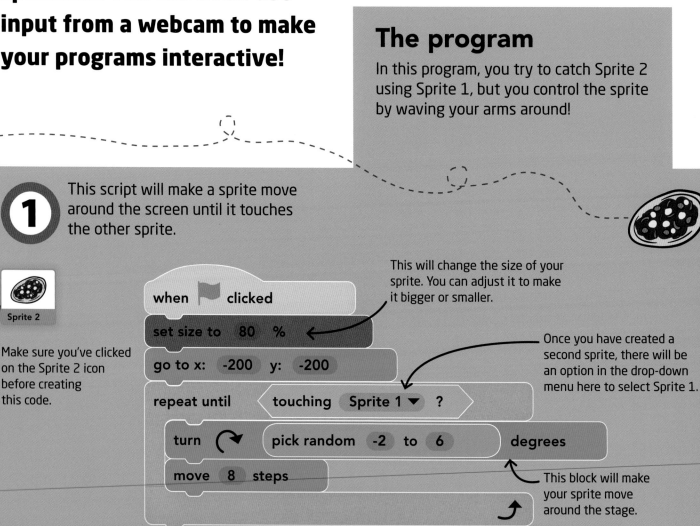

Sprite 2

Make sure you've clicked on the Sprite 2 icon before creating this code.

This will change the size of your sprite. You can adjust it to make it bigger or smaller.

when ⚑ clicked

set size to 80 %

go to x: -200 y: -200

repeat until   touching Sprite 1 ▼ ?

turn ↻ pick random -2 to 6   degrees

move 8 steps

Once you have created a second sprite, there will be an option in the drop-down menu here to select Sprite 1.

This block will make your sprite move around the stage.

2 The script here lets you control the second sprite with movement. The sprite will move in the direction of the motion on the webcam.

Make sure you've clicked on the Sprite 1 icon before creating this code.

Sprite 1

Useful tip

If you find you've written your code for the wrong sprite, don't worry—you don't have to write it all again. Drag the section of code you've already made onto the correct sprite icon underneath the stage and those blocks will be copied over to that sprite.

```
when ⚑ clicked

go to x: 0 y: 0

set size to 80 %

🎥 turn video on ▼

🎥 set video transparency to 50

repeat until < touching Sprite 2 ▼ ? >

    point in direction 🎥 video direction ▼ on sprite ▼

    move 5 steps

say You got it! for 2 seconds

🎥 turn video off ▼
```

This block will let you see yourself on the stage, but slightly faded so you can still see the sprites, too.

This block makes Sprite 2 turn toward any movement on the stage.

Don't forget to add code to turn the camera off once Sprite 1 catches Sprite 2.

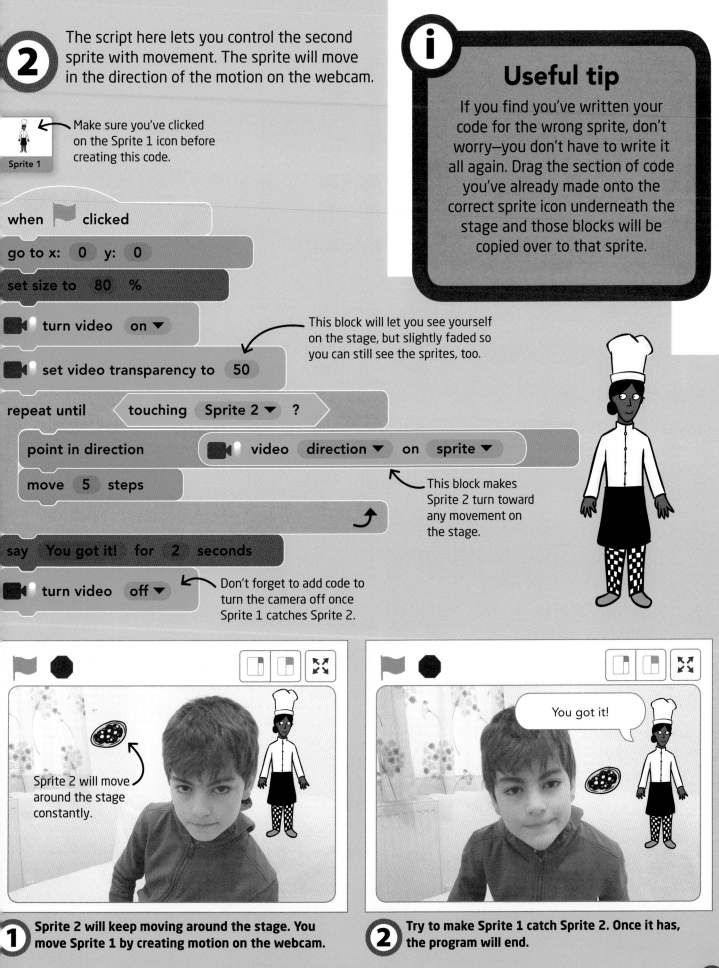

Sprite 2 will move around the stage constantly.

You got it!

1 Sprite 2 will keep moving around the stage. You move Sprite 1 by creating motion on the webcam.

2 Try to make Sprite 1 catch Sprite 2. Once it has, the program will end.

Collisions

When a sprite runs into the edge of the stage, or another sprite, that's a collision! A collision happens whenever two objects touch. In some games, you want two objects to collide, but in others you want to avoid collisions!

Make a collision

Collisions are recognized in Scratch by "touching" condition blocks. If you want to check whether two things are colliding at a specific moment, or if you want to have something happen any time two things collide, put the "touching" block inside a conditional block.

> touching edge ▼ ?

This condition asks if the sprite is touching the edge of the stage.

The program

In this game, a princess has to avoid a horde of dragons! Can you help her escape them? First, we need to make a flying dragon that copies, or "clones," itself when it goes off the edge of the stage. That way we don't have to keep making new sprites.

1 This code makes a dragon move across the screen until it hits the edge of the stage. The dragon then deletes itself, but makes a new dragon start at the beginning.

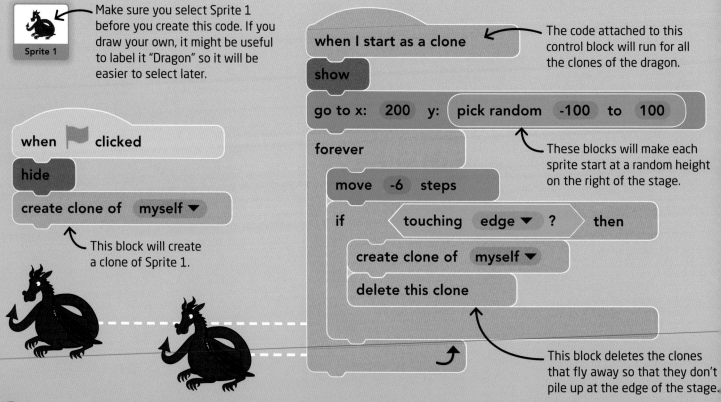

Sprite 1

Make sure you select Sprite 1 before you create this code. If you draw your own, it might be useful to label it "Dragon" so it will be easier to select later.

```
when ⚑ clicked
hide
create clone of  myself ▼
```

This block will create a clone of Sprite 1.

```
when I start as a clone
show
go to x:  200  y:  pick random  -100  to  100
forever
    move  -6  steps
    if        touching  edge ▼  ?        then
        create clone of  myself ▼
        delete this clone
```

The code attached to this control block will run for all the clones of the dragon.

These blocks will make each sprite start at a random height on the right of the stage.

This block deletes the clones that fly away so that they don't pile up at the edge of the stage.

2 This code lets you control the princess, but also makes her say "Ouch!" or "Oops!" if she collides with a dragon or with the edge of the stage.

Select Sprite 2 before creating this code.

Sprite 2

```
when [flag] clicked
show
point in direction 90
go to x: -100 y: 0
set size to 80 %
forever
    change y by -3
    if < touching Sprite 1 ▼ ? > then
        say Ouch! for 1 seconds
        hide
        stop all ▼
    if < touching edge ▼ ? > then
        say Oops! for 1 seconds
        hide
        stop all ▼
```

```
when space ▼ key pressed
change y by 40
```

Sprite 2 starts on the left of the stage.

This line adds gravity to your game, making Sprite 2 fall a little all the time.

This bit of code moves Sprite 2 toward the top of the screen. You need to keep pressing the space bar to stop her from falling.

i

Useful tip

In order to select another sprite from the drop-down menu in the "touching" blocks, they must already be added to the Sprite List. Make sure you add all the sprites you want before you start writing your code.

The code sets Sprite 2's size to 80%. You can play around with that number to see what size is the most fun!

Ouch!

If the princess collides with the dragon, the game is over.

Oops!

The game will also end if the princess collides with any of the stage's edges.

Variables

Sometimes you need to keep track of things that change in a program or game. You can do this using variables. A variable is a placeholder that can be used for a value, even if the value changes while the program is running. Variables are really useful for keeping score in a game.

Create a variable block

You can create your own variables in Scratch. Here's how to create a variable to keep track of the score in a game. You'll find what you need in the Variables section.

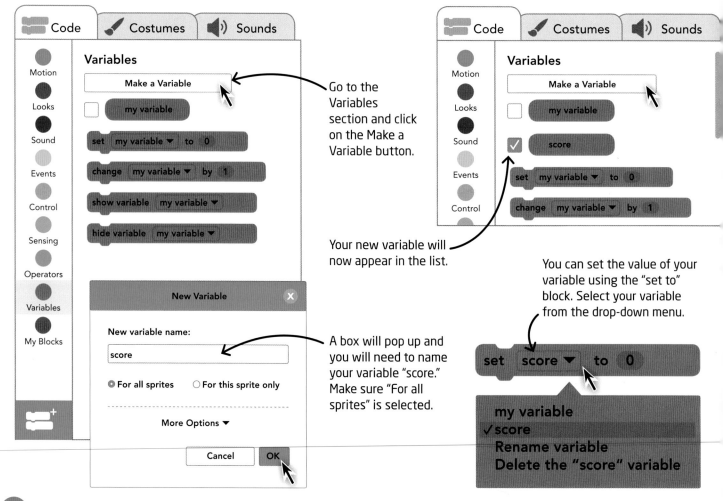

Go to the Variables section and click on the Make a Variable button.

Your new variable will now appear in the list.

A box will pop up and you will need to name your variable "score." Make sure "For all sprites" is selected.

You can set the value of your variable using the "set to" block. Select your variable from the drop-down menu.

The program

In this game, we'll make hearts keep falling down. A variable will make the score go up if a llama catches them or down if the llama misses them.

1 This code makes a heart sprite move across the stage. It will add 1 to the score if it touches the llama or -1 if the heart gets to the bottom of the stage.

Sprite 1

```
when ⚑ clicked
set score ▼ to 0
show
create clone of myself ▼
hide
```

When you start the program, the score will be set to 0.

```
when I start as a clone
set size to 30 %
go to x: pick random -150 to 150   y: 150
forever
    change y by -8
    if        touching Sprite 2 ▼ ?        then
        change score ▼ by 1
        create clone of myself ▼
        delete this clone

    if        touching edge ▼ ?        then
        change score ▼ by -1
        create clone of myself ▼
        delete this clone
```

Choose Sprite 2 from the drop-down menu.

This block will add a value of 1 to your variable every time Sprite 2 touches Sprite 1.

This block will minus a value of 1 from your variable every time Sprite 2 misses Sprite 1.

2 These blocks of code let you move the llama left and right.

Sprite 2

```
when ⚑ clicked
set size to 55 %
go to x: 0   y: -100
point in direction 90
```

```
when right arrow ▼ key pressed
move 15 steps
```

This code will move Sprite 2 right when you click the right arrow.

```
when left arrow ▼ key pressed
move -15 steps
```

This code will move Sprite 2 left when you click the left arrow.

Your variable "score" will appear in the top left of the stage.

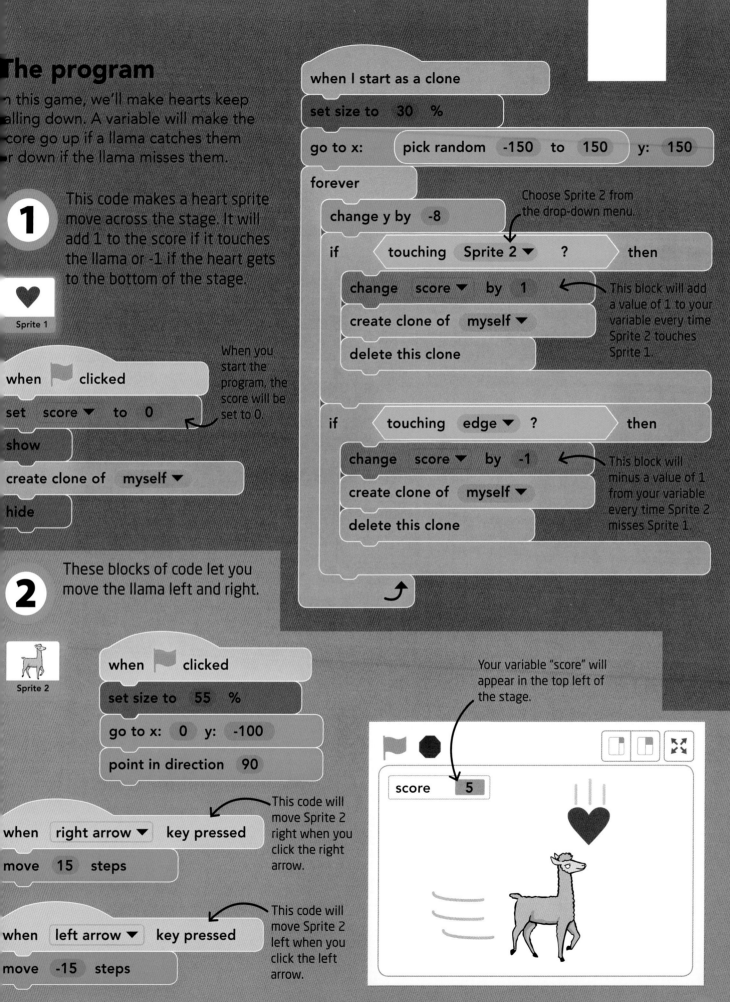

score 5

109

Satoru Iwata

Video-game programmer • Born 1959
• From Japan

Satoru Iwata always loved playing video games. From an early age, he was fascinated with how games were created and developed. He went on to become president of Nintendo, a worldwide video game and electronics company based in Japan.

Early training

Iwata was still in school when he created his first video game! He made it on a programmable calculator. Iwata went on to study computer science at the Tokyo Institute of Technology. It was there that he learned the skills he needed to develop programming for games.

Nintendo

Iwata helped to program many games for the video-game maker Nintendo. In 2002, he became the fourth president of Nintendo, and he helped launch several new consoles, such as the handheld Nintendo DS and the Nintendo Wii.

Pokémon GO

Iwata was involved in the creation of Pokémon GO—a mobile game where you catch virtual reality creatures called Pokémon. Developed by Nintendo, Niantic, and The Pokémon Company, the game uses a phone camera to make Pokémon appear as if they are in the real world.

Iwata Asks

Iwata hosted video interviews with Nintendo programmers about Nintendo games, hardware, and the coders themselves. This series of videos, called "Iwata Asks," taught fans about how games were created.

Nintendo DS

One of the most popular Nintendo consoles was the handheld Nintendo DS. Iwata oversaw its release in 2004. The DS was unlike previous handheld devices in that it had a split screen and worked using a touchscreen and stylus.

Functions

What do you do when you want to run the same bit of code several times but you want to do something else in between? Then it's time for a function! Functions let you name a special section of code that you want to use later. Then, when you want that code in a program, you can just use your named block!

Make a function block

As with a variable, you have to create a function block before you can use it in a program. The code for a function has two parts: the definition block and the name block. You can make a function in the "My Blocks" section. Here, we'll create a function that makes a sprite draw a triangle.

To complete your function, add the code that you want below the "define" block. You can then use the block in your program.

```
define    draw a triangle
```
```
     pen down
```
```
repeat  3
     move  70  steps
     turn  ↻  120  degrees
```
```
     pen up
```

You can find the pen tools in Add Extension.

Give your function a name that describes it so that you can remember what it does when you want to use it later.

Code   Costumes   Sounds

My Blocks

Motion

Looks
Make a Block

Sound
draw a triangle

Events

Control
Click on Make a Block and a pop-up window will appear.

Sensing

Operators

Variable

My Blocks

Pen

Make a Block

🗑

Block name

Add an input number or text	Add an input boolean	text Add a label

○ Run without screen refresh

Cancel   OK

When you have named your block, click OK.

```
when  ⚑  clicked
draw a triangle
```

The program

Functions are useful when you need to repeat any section of code more than once, but they are really powerful when you use them several times in the same program. Here, we will use the triangle function over and over to make some beautiful designs.

This is your triangle, drawn 12 times in a circle.

```
when 🏳 clicked

    🖊 erase all

go to x: -80  y: 0

point in direction 90

repeat 12

    🖊 set pen color to ⬤

    draw a triangle

    turn ↻ 30 degrees

go to x: 80  y: 0

repeat 8

    🖊 set pen color to ⬤

    draw a triangle

    turn ↻ 45 degrees

go to x: -200  y: -200
```

Make sure to clear the stage before you start so that you have a blank canvas.

Add your function to draw a triangle shape.

There are 360 degrees in a circle. As the loop repeats 12 times, you want each triangle to be drawn a farther 30 degrees around, as there are 12 times 30 degrees in 360.

This is the same triangle, drawn 8 times in a circle.

This block will move the sprite out of the way so that you can see your finished creation!

Now try...

What other drawings can you make with your triangle? What happens if you change the number of repeats and how many degrees the triangle turns in the program?

Functions with parameters

What happens when you want to do something over and over, but not in exactly the same way every time? Then you need a function that you can change—a function with parameters. Parameters are a kind of variable that make your function work differently in different situations.

Make a function with parameter block

We are going to make a block called "draw a square." Select Make a Block and name your function, then select "Add an input" and name the input "size." This input will be our parameter and it will change the size of the square.

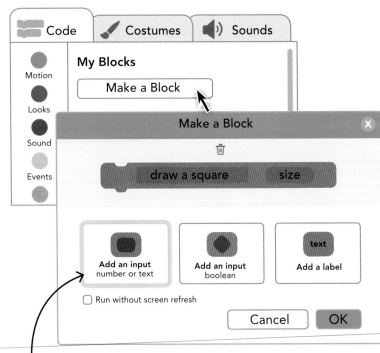

Click "Add an input" to add a parameter to your function.

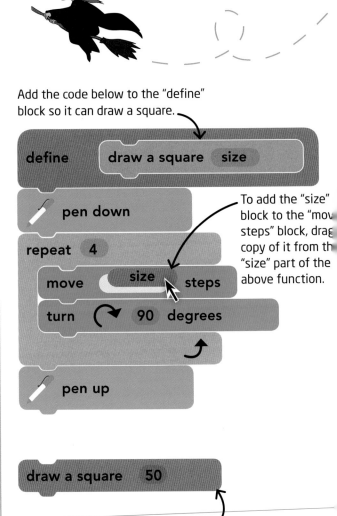

Add the code below to the "define" block so it can draw a square.

To add the "size" block to the "mov steps" block, drag copy of it from th "size" part of the above function.

When you use your "draw a square" function, there is a space for you to fill in a value for the parameter "size."

The program

Now we are going to use our function with parameter block to make a pattern of different squares with variable sizes. Each time we want to make a new square, all we have to do is use our function and add the size of the square that we want to draw.

when ⚑ clicked

erase all

go to x: -30 y: 90

point in direction 90

repeat 10

draw a square 20

move 60 steps

draw a square 55

turn ↻ 36 degrees

go to x: 0 y: 0

repeat 9

draw a square 30

turn ↻ 40 degrees

go to x: -200 y: -200

This function with parameter block draws a square with sides 20 pixels long.

This function with parameter block draws a square with sides 55 pixels long.

This moves the sprite to a new position to start drawing a second circle of squares.

The sprite turns 36 degrees for every repeat. Since there are 360 degrees in a circle, the loop needs to repeat 10 times.

This code draws three different-sized squares. Instead of making three different functions, though, you only need one function with a parameter.

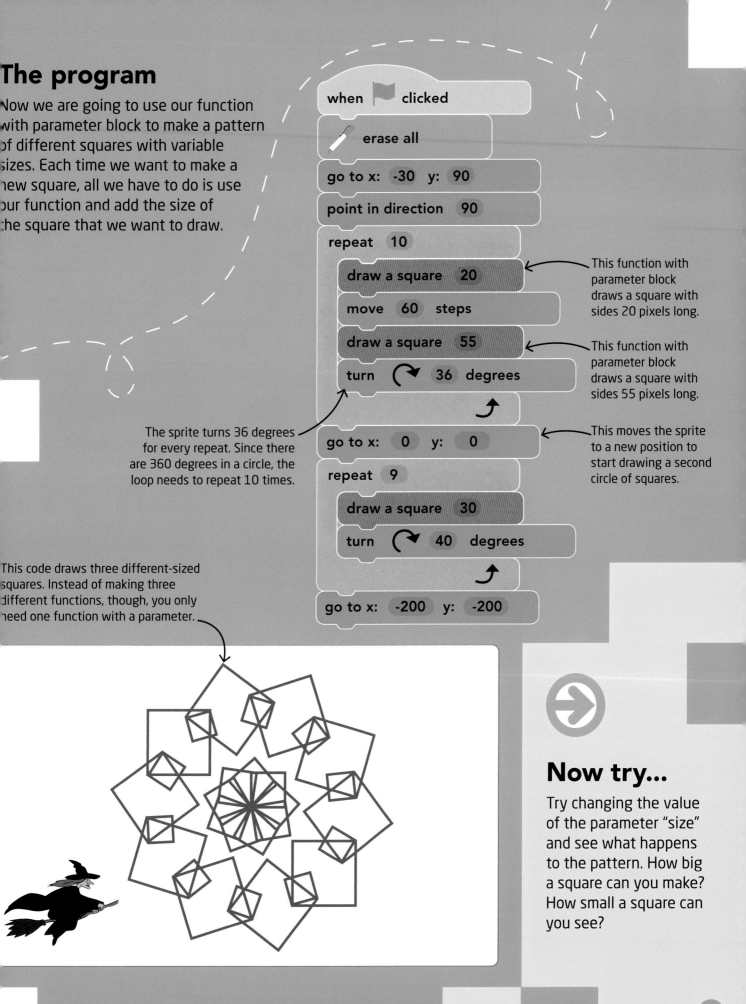

Now try...

Try changing the value of the parameter "size" and see what happens to the pattern. How big a square can you make? How small a square can you see?

Decomposition

Even if you know what you want your program to do, it's not always clear what blocks you'll need or how you will get the computer to complete the actions you want. That's why you need decomposition. When you decompose a problem, you break it down into smaller pieces to see more easily how to program each part.

The algorithm

Here's an algorithm for a program that takes words and spells them backward. It needs to be broken down further before it can be coded. Can you identify which steps can be done with a single block and which parts might need to be decomposed?

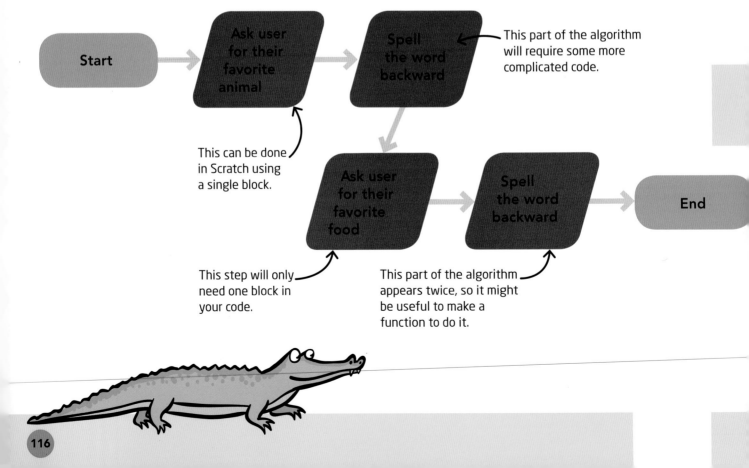

Start → Ask user for their favorite animal → Spell the word backward

This part of the algorithm will require some more complicated code.

This can be done in Scratch using a single block.

Ask user for their favorite food → Spell the word backward → End

This step will only need one block in your code.

This part of the algorithm appears twice, so it might be useful to make a function to do it.

Decomposing your algorithm

There isn't a single block in Scratch that spells a word backward, so this step would benefit from decomposition. Think about this step and what smaller steps within it need to happen. Also, since the step appears twice, you could make a function with parameters to save time later!

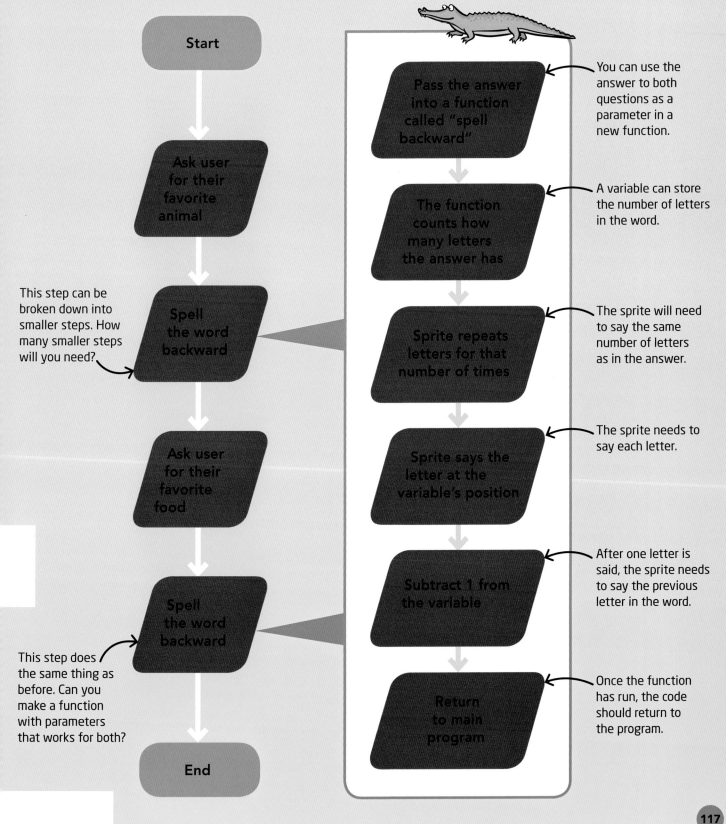

Start

Ask user for their favorite animal

This step can be broken down into smaller steps. How many smaller steps will you need?

Spell the word backward

Ask user for their favorite food

Spell the word backward

This step does the same thing as before. Can you make a function with parameters that works for both?

End

Pass the answer into a function called "spell backward"

You can use the answer to both questions as a parameter in a new function.

The function counts how many letters the answer has

A variable can store the number of letters in the word.

Sprite repeats letters for that number of times

The sprite will need to say the same number of letters as in the answer.

Sprite says the letter at the variable's position

The sprite needs to say each letter.

Subtract 1 from the variable

After one letter is said, the sprite needs to say the previous letter in the word.

Return to main program

Once the function has run, the code should return to the program.

Making new blocks

The decomposed steps need both a variable and a new function. You can create those in the Blocks Palette under Variables and My Blocks. Make sure to name everything in a way that reminds you what your blocks are used for.

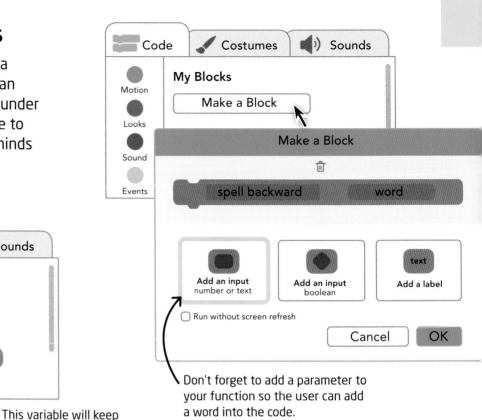

This variable will keep track of the letters in each answer.

Don't forget to add a parameter to your function so the user can add a word into the code.

Defining your function

Now you need to tell your function what to do when it's time to spell a word backward. Try to match the decomposed steps to each block of code.

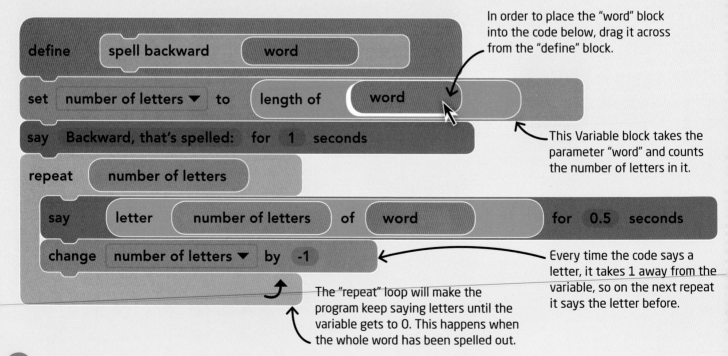

In order to place the "word" block into the code below, drag it across from the "define" block.

This Variable block takes the parameter "word" and counts the number of letters in it.

Every time the code says a letter, it takes 1 away from the variable, so on the next repeat it says the letter before.

The "repeat" loop will make the program keep saying letters until the variable gets to 0. This happens when the whole word has been spelled out.

The program

Now you can build the whole program. When it runs, the sprite will ask the user to enter answers that can then be spelled backward.

```
when [flag] clicked
ask  What's your favorite animal?  and wait
spell backward          answer
ask  What's your favorite food?  and wait
spell backward          answer
```

This Sensing block makes the program wait until the user has typed an answer.

This block will call the function that you defined earlier using the answer from the question above it.

Your variable value will show here if the box beside the variable in the Blocks Palette is checked.

---

numLetters 0

What's your favorite animal?

This box appears automatically when you use an "ask" block.

1 First, the program will ask the user for their favorite animal and a box will appear. Type your answer in and click on the check mark.

---

numLetters 5

Backward, that's spelled:

2 The program counts the number of letters in your answer. If you picked "horse," which has five letters, you will see "5" appear on the stage.

---

numLetters 3

Watch the variable value count down each time the loop runs.

r

The sprite will say each letter one by one.

3 The sprite says each letter of the word from last to first. It stops when the variable gets to 0.

---

numLetters 0

What's your favorite food?

The sprite will now spell your favorite food backward.

4 Once the function has run, the code returns to the main program and asks you the next question.

The program

These scripts make a sprite change costume, color, and size. However, the program is much longer than it needs to be. Take a look at it and see if you can find any repeating patterns that you could replace with a function.

```
when space ▼ key pressed
go to x: 0  y: 0
point in direction 90
switch costume to costume1 ▼
set size to 100 %
clear graphic effects
wait 2 seconds
```

```
when this sprite clicked
go to x: 0  y: 0
point in direction 90
switch costume to costume1 ▼
set size to 100 %
clear graphic effects
stop all ▼
```

```
when ⚑ clicked
go to x: 0  y: 0
point in direction 90
switch costume to costume1 ▼
set size to 100 %
clear graphic effects
wait 2 seconds
forever
    go to random position ▼
    if touching edge ▼ then
        change size by -20
        turn ↻ 15 degrees
        change color ▼ effect by 25
    else
        change size by 20
        turn ↺ 37 degrees

    next costume
    wait 0.5 seconds
```

Pattern matching

Sometimes pieces of code that work for one thing will also work for other similar programs. Looking for patterns in scripts can help you find code that can be reused or made into a function that you can use whenever you need it.

Make a function

There are three places in the scripts where the sprite is sent back to the center of the stage, turned the right way, and reset to its original costume, size, and color. Can you see where? They can all be replaced by a single function.

Define the "reset" function by adding all the code that repeats in all three scripts.

<code> Code | ✏ Costumes | 🔊 Sounds</code>

My Blocks

Motion

Looks

Sound

Events

Control

Sensing

Operators

Variable

My Blocks

Make a Block

reset

Make a new block that will hold the reused code.

Name the block something that will remind you what it does.

Make a Block

🗑

Block name

Add an input
number or text

Add an input
boolean

Add a label

◯ Run without screen refresh

Cancel   OK

Press OK when you're done.

define   reset

go to x: 0   y: 0

point in direction 90

switch costume to   costume1 ▼

set size to   100   %

clear graphic effects

All these blocks are repeated in the same order in the scripts.

reset

All three scripts can now start with the new function.

Now try...

What if you don't want to position your sprite in the center each time? Can you add a parameter to your "reset" function so that you can start your sprite in a different location each time you use your function?

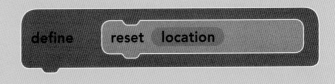

define   reset location

Three functions

Before you create the program, make these three functions in Scratch. Each one sets the sprite to be a different size and color.

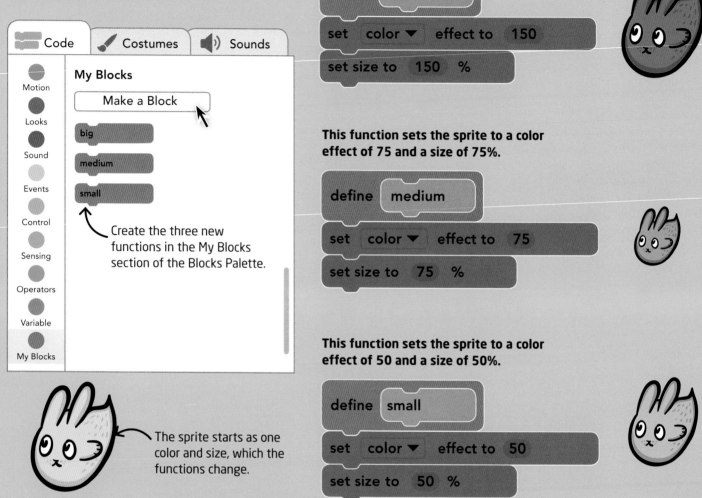

This function sets the sprite to a color effect of 150 and a size of 150%.

```
define big

set color ▼ effect to 150
set size to 150 %
```

This function sets the sprite to a color effect of 75 and a size of 75%.

```
define medium

set color ▼ effect to 75
set size to 75 %
```

This function sets the sprite to a color effect of 50 and a size of 50%.

```
define small

set color ▼ effect to 50
set size to 50 %
```

Code **Costumes** **Sounds**

Motion
Looks
Sound
Events
Control
Sensing
Operators
Variable
My Blocks

My Blocks

Make a Block

big

medium

small

Create the three new functions in the My Blocks section of the Blocks Palette.

The sprite starts as one color and size, which the functions change.

Abstraction

When you look at something that has too much detail, you can lose the big idea underneath. In this program, we'll give you three different functions. Your job is to take away the unnecessary details that could be added as parameters later. Making code simpler like this is called abstraction.

he program

he program makes the sprite big, then
mall, then medium-sized, and changes
:s color each time.

1

he functions here change the size
nd color of the sprite, with pauses in
etween each change so you can see
hem happen.

```
when    clicked

big

wait   1   seconds

small

wait   1   seconds

medium
```

First the sprite
grows bigger, then it
shrinks to be small.

The "wait" blocks
make the code slow
enough for you to
see the color and
size changes.

At the end the
sprite grows to be
medium-sized.

2

ou don't really need three
eparate functions to make
ne program work—and
unctions take time to make.
nstead, you can make one
unction with parameters!

```
define    abstracted function   change

set   color ▼   effect to        change

set size to       change      %
```

```
when    clicked

abstracted function   150

wait   1   seconds

abstracted function   50

wait   1   seconds

abstracted function   75
```

Remember you can drag
the "change" parameter
here directly from the
"define" block above.

Now you can use the
same function to add
in the size and color
change effect values
you want.

123

Bill Gates

Programmer and businessman
● Born 1955 ● From the USA

Bill Gates is the cofounder of the world-famous computer company Microsoft. Gates learned to code at an early age and went on to create hugely successful software. Today, he and his wife are well-known for the charity work they do.

By the 1990s, Microsoft's Windows operating system had become the preferred choice for PCs.

BASIC for Altair 8800

One of the most popular personal computers (PCs) in the 1970s was the Altair 8800. Gates and his childhood friend Paul Allen created a program called a compiler that allowed the Altair to be programmed with BASIC

Early training

It was not common for schools to have computers when Gates was young. He was lucky enough to have access to one and wrote a computer program to play tic-tac-toe on it. He used an early version of BASIC, a programming language that was popular at the time.

Altair 8800 computer

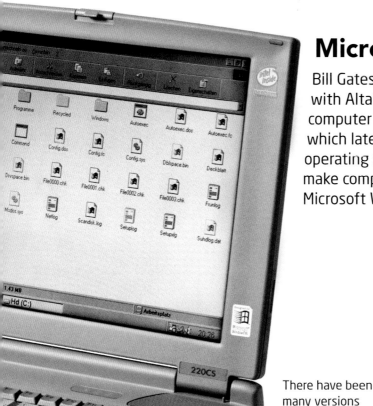

Micro-Soft

Bill Gates and Paul Allen found great success with Altair BASIC. They continued to develop computer software under the name Micro-Soft, which later became Microsoft. They also created operating systems, which are the programs that make computers work. The operating system Microsoft Windows is now used around the world.

There have been many versions of the Windows operating system.

Harvard University

After high school, Gates attended Harvard University in Massachusetts, where he studied both mathematics and computer science. He chose to drop out of Harvard, however, so he could concentrate on making and selling software.

Charity work

In 2000, Bill Gates and his wife, Melinda, set up a charity called the Bill & Melinda Gates Foundation. Its goals include improving education and health, particularly in poorer communities. Bill and Melinda received the Presidential Medal of Freedom for their work. This is one of the top awards given to US citizens who have made an important impact on society.

Bill and Melinda Gates were awarded the Presidential Medal of Freedom by US president Barack Obama in 2016.

Remixing

When you remix a project, you take something that's already been created and change it or add to it so that it works better for you. Remixing can be a form of collaboration or it can be a way to add variety to a project that you have made yourself.

The program

Here is a program that lets you move sprites around and create patterns using a webcam. Can you use the skills you've learned in this book to remix the program and make it even better?

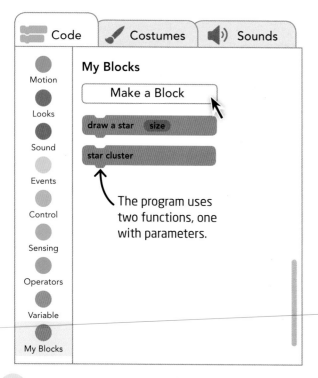

The program uses two functions, one with parameters.

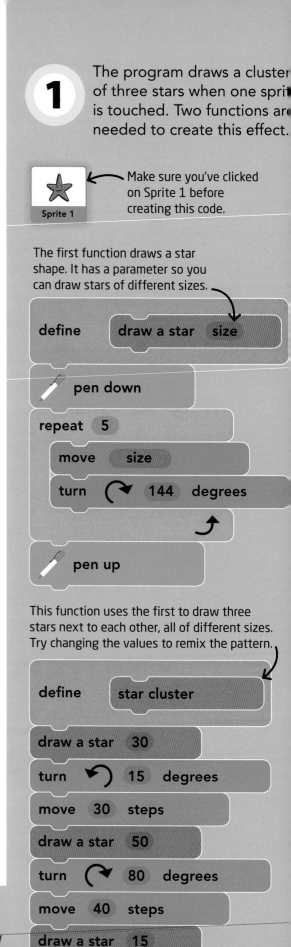

1 The program draws a cluster of three stars when one sprite is touched. Two functions are needed to create this effect.

Make sure you've clicked on Sprite 1 before creating this code.

The first function draws a star shape. It has a parameter so you can draw stars of different sizes.

This function uses the first to draw three stars next to each other, all of different sizes. Try changing the values to remix the pattern.

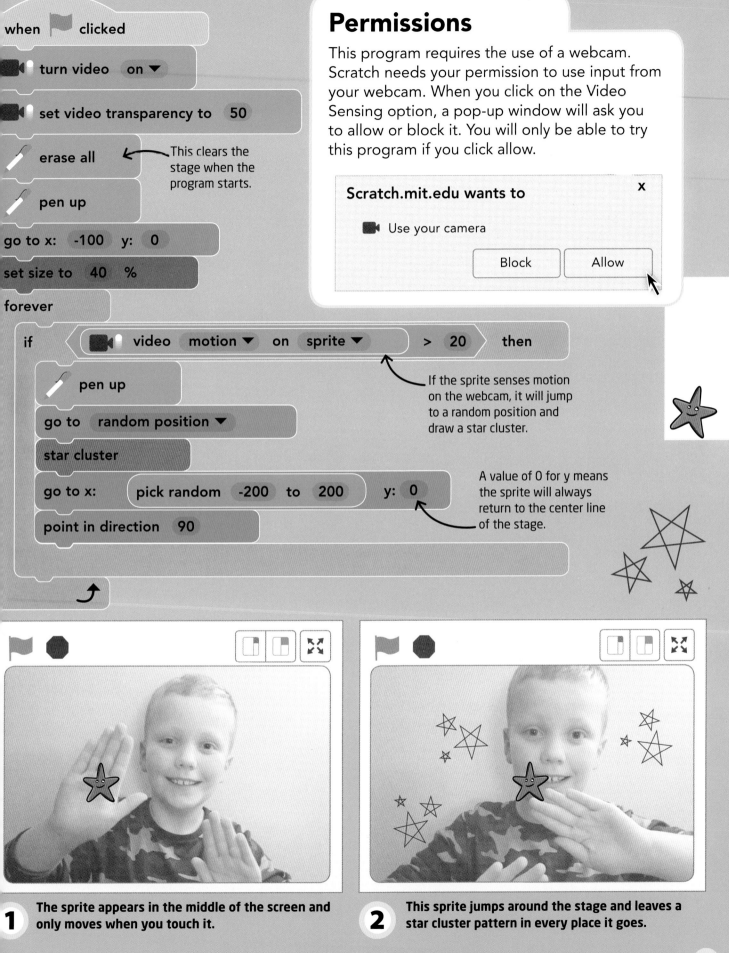

when 🏳 clicked

📹 turn video on ▼

📹 set video transparency to 50

✏ erase all ← This clears the stage when the program starts.

✏ pen up

go to x: -100 y: 0

set size to 40 %

forever

if ⟨ 📹 video motion ▼ on sprite ▼ > 20 ⟩ then

✏ pen up

go to random position ▼

star cluster

go to x: pick random -200 to 200 y: 0

point in direction 90

If the sprite senses motion on the webcam, it will jump to a random position and draw a star cluster.

A value of 0 for y means the sprite will always return to the center line of the stage.

Permissions

This program requires the use of a webcam. Scratch needs your permission to use input from your webcam. When you click on the Video Sensing option, a pop-up window will ask you to allow or block it. You will only be able to try this program if you click allow.

Scratch.mit.edu wants to ✕

📹 Use your camera

Block | Allow

1 The sprite appears in the middle of the screen and only moves when you touch it.

2 This sprite jumps around the stage and leaves a star cluster pattern in every place it goes.

2 The second sprite in the program makes a stamp of itself in a different size each time you hit it. You could remix it to make more or fewer stamps, or to change its color every time.

Sprite 2

Make sure you've clicked on Sprite 2 before creating this code.

```
when 🏴 clicked
go to x: 100 y: 0
set size to 100 %
```
Change the size of the sprite if you want to.

The sprite will only make a stamp if it senses enough motion on the webcam.

```
forever
    if ◀ 🎥 video motion ▼ on sprite ▼ > 20 ▶ then
        🖊 pen up
        go to random position ▼
        next costume
        set size to pick random 10 to 200 %
        set ghost ▼ effect to 50
        🖊 stamp
        set ghost ▼ effect to 0
        set size to 100 %
        go to x: pick random -200 to 200 y: 0
```

Make sure to pick a sprite with more than one costume.

The "ghost" effect will make the sprite a little see-through before it stamps.

This will leave a copy of the sprite's image wherever you use it.

After making a stamp, the sprite will return to the center line of the screen.

ⓘ

Useful tip

Whenever you create a program that makes a sprite change costume, make sure you've picked a sprite that has more than one costume already. Alternatively, you can make extra costumes for the sprite yourself.

3 The final sprite deletes everything on the screen when you collide with it. This one will clear the screen when it gets too messy.

X
Sprite 3

Make sure you've clicked on Sprite 3 before creating this code.

```
when ⚑ clicked
go to x: 0  y: 0
set size to 70 %
forever
    if < 📹 video motion ▼ on sprite ▼ > 20 > then
        ✎ pen up
        go to random position ▼
        ✎ erase all
        go to x: pick random -200 to 200  y: 0
        point in direction 90
```

A "forever" block means the following code will run anytime you collide with the sprite, not just the first time.

This sprite will delete all the star clusters and stamps on the screen when it is touched.

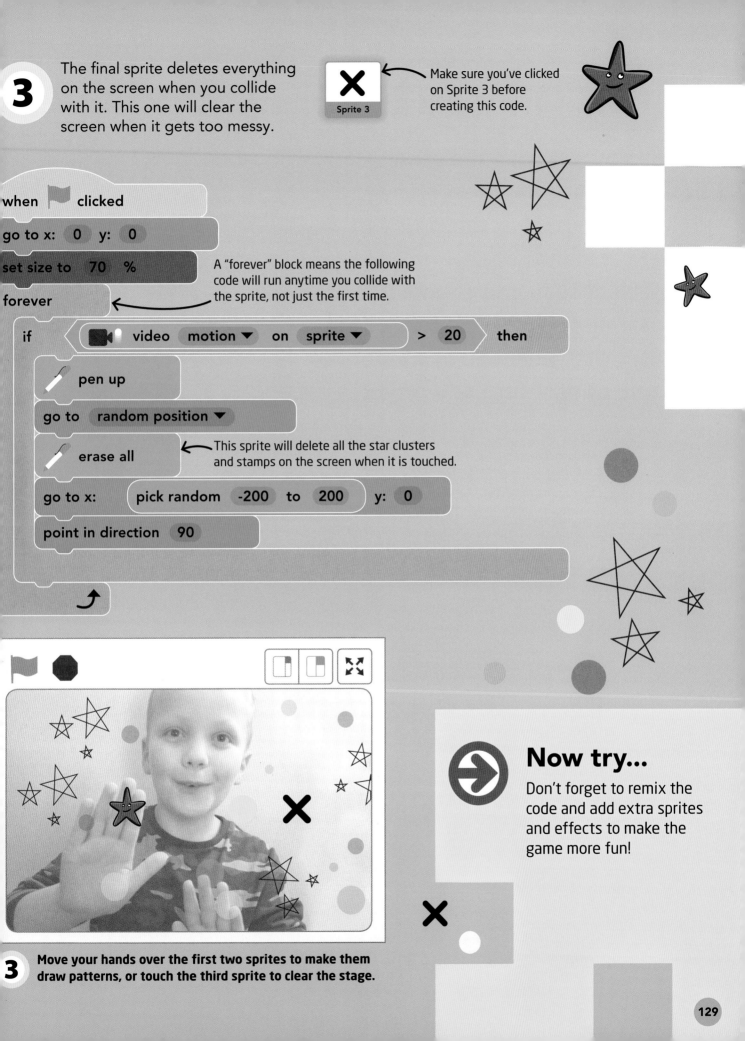

Now try...

Don't forget to remix the code and add extra sprites and effects to make the game more fun!

3 Move your hands over the first two sprites to make them draw patterns, or touch the third sprite to clear the stage.

Minicomputers

Minicomputers have the same basic parts as computers many times their size, but these tiny devices are small enough to fit in the palm of someone's hand. Despite their small size, they have all of the features that you need to create amazing things—such as a robot!

DIY robot

Marty is a robot that comes in a kit to be made at home. It can be controlled by a Raspberry Pi using the programming languages Scratch, Python, or JavaScript. Marty can be programmed to walk and dance.

micro:bit

The micro:bit has built-in LED lights and buttons. Once it is programmed, you can play games on it without any extra attachments.

These chips might seem tiny but they're very powerful.

Battery pack connectors let you play the games you make anywhere!

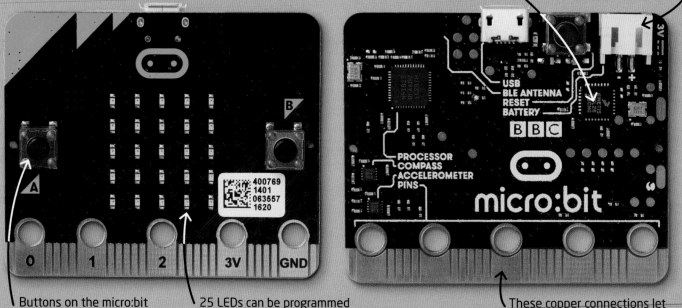

USB
BLE ANTENNA
RESET
BATTERY

PROCESSOR
COMPASS
ACCELEROMETER
PINS

BBC

micro:bit

Buttons on the micro:bit allow you to give it input while a program is running.

25 LEDs can be programmed to display letters, numbers, or pictures.

These copper connections let you attach and program other devices, such as a speaker.

Raspberry Pi

A Raspberry Pi can be used to program anything from a touch-screen tablet to a humanoid robot, depending on which pieces of hardware are attached to it.

Two USB ports are used to connect devices, the same way you would connect devices to your home computer.

input and output pins let you add hardware.

This little chip is in charge of the USB ports, as well as the ethernet port.

The Raspberry Pi has built-in Wi-Fi, but it also comes with an ethernet port so you can connect to the internet with a cable.

A power supply can be connected by micro USB.

The audio jack connection and HDMI slot allow you to connect screens and speakers.

Arduino

An Arduino, like a micro:bit, is programmed using another computer. They can only store a single program at a time.

There are 14 digital pins that let you connect input and output devices.

Uno is just one type of Arduino.

The Arduino connects to a computer with a USB cable to program it the way you want it.

This board lets you choose multiple power options, depending on the power that your devices need.

The barrel jack connection lets you connect a battery and run your programs without access to electricity.

How to connect micro:bit

In order to use Scratch to program a micro:bit, you need to do a couple of things before you start. This section will tell you what you need to know.

Requirements:

 Windows 10 version 1709+ or mac OS 10.13+

Bluetooth 4.0

Scratch Link

1 **Install Scratch Link and micro:bit HEX**
Ask an adult for permission to download and install Scratch Link and micro:bit HEX. Both applications can be found at:
https://scratch.mit.edu/microbit
Follow the instructions provided.

2 **Connect micro:bit to Scratch**
Make sure the micro:bit is still connected to your computer via the USB cable in order to begin programming it.

3 **Add the micro:bit extension**
When you open Scratch, add the micro:bit extension to the Blocks Palette.

micro:bit

Scratch has special blocks that let you write code for other devices, such as the micro:bit. The micro:bit is a minicomputer that has buttons and lights built into it. You can use it to create fun games!

The program

This program will make your micro:bit into a controller for a game in Scratch. You will be able to use the buttons to make the sprite jump. The micro:bit will even display your score!

1 First, we'll code our main sprite. These scripts will reset the game when you start it, define how you win or lose, and let you control the main sprite.

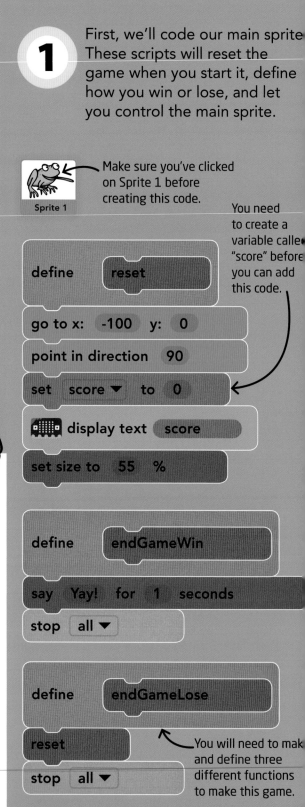

Sprite 1

Make sure you've clicked on Sprite 1 before creating this code.

You need to create a variable called "score" before you can add this code.

```
define   reset

go to x:  -100   y:  0

point in direction  90

set  score ▼  to  0

🔲 display text  score

set size to  55  %
```

```
define   endGameWin

say  Yay!  for  1  seconds

stop  all ▼
```

```
define   endGameLose

reset

stop  all ▼
```

You will need to make and define three different functions to make this game.

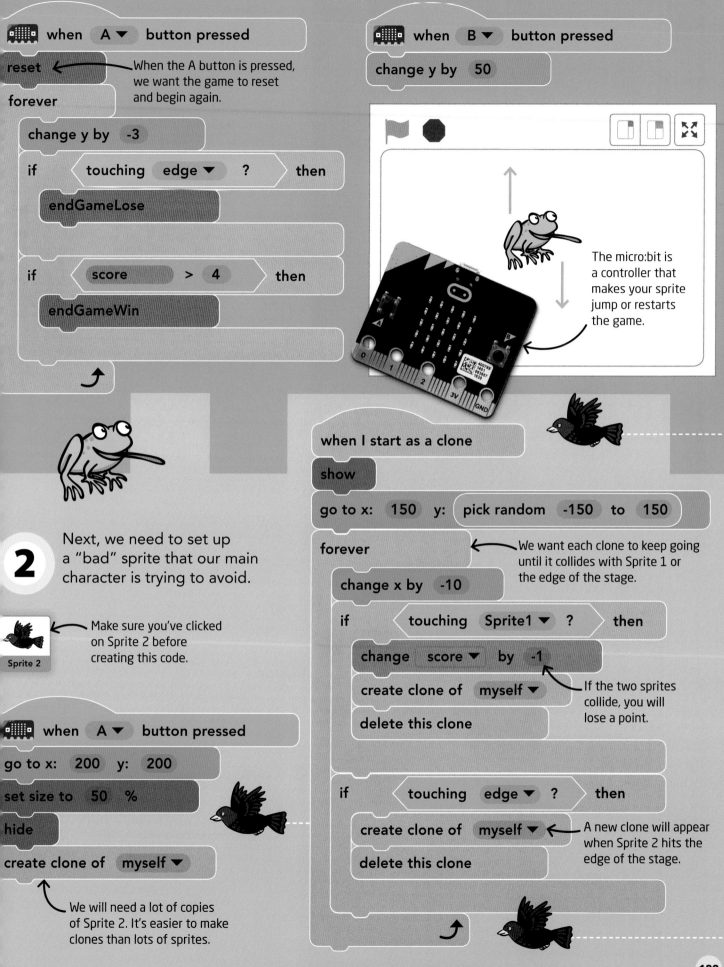

when A ▾ **button pressed**

reset ← When the A button is pressed, we want the game to reset and begin again.

forever

> change y by -3
>
> **if** ⟨ touching edge ▾ ? ⟩ **then**
>
> > endGameLose
>
> **if** ⟨ score > 4 ⟩ **then**
>
> > endGameWin

when B ▾ **button pressed**

change y by 50

The micro:bit is a controller that makes your sprite jump or restarts the game.

2 Next, we need to set up a "bad" sprite that our main character is trying to avoid.

Sprite 2 — Make sure you've clicked on Sprite 2 before creating this code.

when A ▾ **button pressed**

go to x: 200 y: 200

set size to 50 %

hide

create clone of myself ▾

← We will need a lot of copies of Sprite 2. It's easier to make clones than lots of sprites.

when I start as a clone

show

go to x: 150 y: pick random -150 to 150

forever ← We want each clone to keep going until it collides with Sprite 1 or the edge of the stage.

> change x by -10
>
> **if** ⟨ touching Sprite1 ▾ ? ⟩ **then**
>
> > change score ▾ by -1 ← If the two sprites collide, you will lose a point.
> >
> > create clone of myself ▾
> >
> > delete this clone
>
> **if** ⟨ touching edge ▾ ? ⟩ **then**
>
> > create clone of myself ▾ ← A new clone will appear when Sprite 2 hits the edge of the stage.
> >
> > delete this clone

3 Finally, we need to write the code for the sprite that you want your main sprite to try to catch to increase your score.

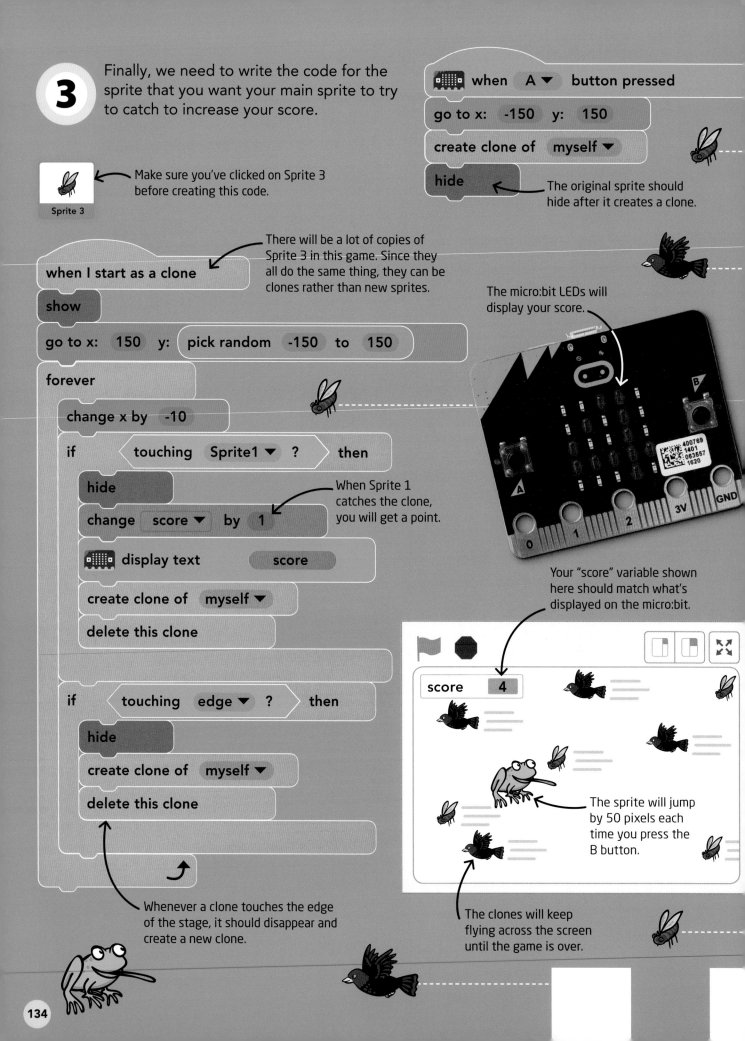

Make sure you've clicked on Sprite 3 before creating this code.

Sprite 3

```
when A ▼ button pressed
go to x: -150  y: 150
create clone of myself ▼
hide
```

The original sprite should hide after it creates a clone.

There will be a lot of copies of Sprite 3 in this game. Since they all do the same thing, they can be clones rather than new sprites.

```
when I start as a clone
show
go to x: 150  y: pick random -150 to 150
forever
    change x by -10
    if    touching Sprite1 ▼ ?    then
        hide
        change score ▼ by 1
        display text        score
        create clone of myself ▼
        delete this clone

    if    touching edge ▼ ?    then
        hide
        create clone of myself ▼
        delete this clone
```

When Sprite 1 catches the clone, you will get a point.

The micro:bit LEDs will display your score.

Your "score" variable shown here should match what's displayed on the micro:bit.

score   4

The sprite will jump by 50 pixels each time you press the B button.

Whenever a clone touches the edge of the stage, it should disappear and create a new clone.

The clones will keep flying across the screen until the game is over.

Answers

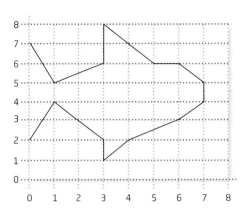

17 **Paper pixels**
Here is what your finished pixel image should look like. It's a dinosaur!

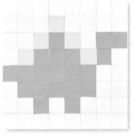

21 **Debugging drawings**
The correct instructions for Box 4 should read: Go diagonally up to 6,6 then across to 5,6 and then diagonally to 3,8. Go to 3,6 and then diagonally down to 1,5. Finish at 0,7.

57 **Parameter path**
This is how to complete the maze. The finished program should look like the blocks below:

56 **Parameter path**
This is how to complete the maze. The finished program should look like the blocks below:

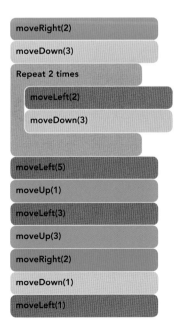

```
moveRight(2)
moveDown(3)
Repeat 2 times
    moveLeft(2)
    moveDown(3)
moveLeft(5)
moveUp(1)
moveLeft(3)
moveUp(3)
moveRight(2)
moveDown(1)
moveLeft(1)
```

```
moveDown(3)
moveLeft(4)
moveDown(2)
moveRight(3)
Repeat 2 times
    moveDown(5)
    moveRight(1)
moveDown(2)
moveRight(2)
moveUp(3)
moveRight(4)
Repeat 2 times
    moveUp(2)
    moveLeft(1)
moveUp(3)
moveLeft(2)
moveDown(2)
```

63 **Pattern matching creepy-crawlies**
These are the things each set of creepy-crawlies has in common:

Arachnids

Which of these things do they have in common?
(Eight legs)
Wings
(A head and body)
Scaly skin
(A hard outer skeleton)

Insects

Which of these things do they have in common?
(Two antennae)
A furry tail
(Wings)
(Six legs)
A long neck

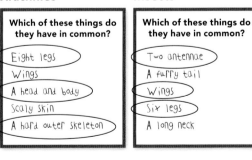

Earwig: Insect
Ant: Insect
Centipede: Neither! It is actually an animal called a myriapod.

Did you know?

There is so much more to computer science than just programming. Computer science has a relatively short history but a lot has happened in that time!

Debugging

In 1946, after noticing that a program was producing bad results, the team working on the ENIAC computer found a moth stuck inside it. Admiral Grace Murray Hopper taped the moth into her notebook, commenting that it was the first "actual case" of a bug being found in code.

Malware

Sometimes people write bad code to try to steal information or stop your machine from working. These programs are known as malware.

Trojan horse This is a bad program disguised as a good one. Once you install it, it can help people steal your data.

Virus A computer virus is a lot like a human virus, copying itself and infecting other programs without permission.

Backdoor programs These programs allow someone to access your machine without a password.

Vulnerability scanners Some people are able to run scanners on systems to find the insecure places where they can get in.

Sniffers As your information passes through the internet, sniffers can inspect each item looking for important data.

Worms A computer worm is a small piece of destructive code that can spread from computer to computer.

Keylogging Criminals can install keyloggers on other people's computers to record the keys they press, in order to steal data.

Fun fact

One of the first computer viruses was written in 1982 as a joke by 15-year-old American Rich Skrenta. He made a virus called Elk Cloner, which made a poem appear on the screen of infected Apple II computers.

Early computers

1

Pascaline mechanical calculator Created by Frenchman Blaise Pascal in 1642, this machine could add and subtract.

2

Konrad Zuse's Z3 Presented in Germany in 1941, some think this is the first example of a reprogrammable computer.

3

Manchester Baby Considered small for its day, this English machine was built in 1948 to test random access memory (RAM).

4

Electronic Numerical Integrator and Computer Finished in 1945, the ENIAC performed complex calculations, but it could take days to program.

5

IBM 360 First sold in 1965, this series of machines could all run the same software, so they could be easily upgraded.

6

TRS-80 By 1977, the TRS-80 had become a popular personal computer. It had a keyboard and could run games.

What a difference!

Colossal computer
In the 1950s, IBM built the SAGE system— a series of connected computers each weighing in at 250 tons (225 metric tons).

Miniature machine
In 2018, IBM produced a computer that is smaller than a grain of salt, but more powerful than the desktop computers of the 1990s. Two are fitted to the motherboard shown here.

Binary

Almost all modern computers use the binary system to send and store data. Information is converted into 1s and 0s, which the computer can change into electronic signals.

Data measurements

File sizes are usually measured in terms of bytes. A byte is a unit about the size of what it takes to store a single letter, number, or symbol. Large amounts of data have their own names.

1 Bit = Single Binary Digit (1 or 0)
1 Byte = 8 Bits
1 Kilobyte (KB) = 1,024 Bytes
1 Megabyte (MB) = 1,024 KB
1 Gigabyte (GB) = 1,024 MB
1 Terabyte (TB) = 1,024 GB
1 Petabyte (PB) = 1,024 TB
1 Exabyte (EB) = 1,024 PB

Glossary

abstraction Making something more simple by removing details

algorithm List of steps that tells you how to do something

artificial intelligence (AI) Ability of a computer to do tasks that usually only a human can do, such as think or learn

block Puzzlelike piece of code that can be dragged into a program

block-based programming Graphical computer language that lets users connect blocks to build code

bug Mistake in a program or algorithm

click Press of the mouse button one time

code Programmed instructions that tell a computer what to do

coder Someone who writes code

coding Writing code

collaboration Working together

collision When two objects touch

computational thinking Solving problems the way a computer would solve them

computer Machine that takes in information and processes it. It has an option to store this information or send something back out

computer language Special kind of language that a computer can understand

computer science Study of the use of computers for solving problems

condition Statement that must be true in order for something to happen

conditional Code that checks whether something is true or false before it proceeds

creativity Ability to produce different and new ideas

data Pieces of information

debugging Finding and fixing bugs

decomposition Taking a problem and breaking it down into pieces that are easier to understand

define (a function) Writing code that tells a computer what a function should do

download File copied to your computer from the internet

double-click Clicking the mouse button twice, quickly

drag Holding the mouse button down as you move it across the screen

drop Releasing the mouse button after dragging something

event Coded trigger that causes other code to start running

fiber-optic cable Cable that sends data using light

forever loop Control block in Scratch that repeats code over and over until the program ends

function Named section of code that can be reused

games console Computer designed to run games, played using controllers

green flag Flag symbol above the Scratch stage that is often used to start programs

hardware Any part of a computer that you can touch

hacker Person who writes code designed to find safety flaws in computers

hat block Any of the blocks that you can use to start a new script in Scratch

if statement Set of code that only runs if a condition is true

if/else statement Set of code where one section runs if a condition is true and a second section runs if the condition is false

input Information sent to the computer or program, such as mouse-clicks, key presses, or movements picked up by a camera

instruction Line of code or command

internet Set of interconnected computers that allow people to communicate across the world

loop Code that repeats over and over again

malware Code designed to steal information or damage a computer

minicomputer Computer that is tiny but has power similar to a full-size machine

online Using the internet

output Information put out by the computer or program, such as words, images, or sounds

parameter Extra piece of information that some functions need to work

pattern Something that's shared between two or more things

pattern matching Recognizing and finding patterns

PC Shortened name for a personal computer

persistence Determination to try something over and over until you succeed

pixel Tiny single-colored square or dot that is part of a bigger image. The Scratch stage is measured in pixels

program Complete section of code that performs a task

programmer Someone who writes programs

programming Writing programs

programming language Language that a programmer uses to write code

remixing Creating a new version of a project that already exists

repeat Do the same thing again

resilience Determination to keep going even when something is hard

run Start a program

robot Machine that independently takes actions based on information that it collects

script Name used for a set of code

software Programs that operate on a computer or machine

sprite Computer image that can be controlled with code

stage Part of the screen where sprites appear in Scratch

statement Complete piece of code that makes a computer do something

username Made-up name that refers to a specific user

value Number, word, or other piece of information, including answers given in Scratch in response to "ask" blocks

variable Placeholder that can be used to refer to information whose value isn't known at the time of programming

website Page of information that can be found online

Wi-Fi Way of sending information from one place to another without wires

World Wide Web Network of computers that talk to each other using an agreed-upon language

USB cable Wire that connects different pieces of hardware that have a USB (Universal Serial Bus) connector

x position Position of a sprite on a horizontal axis

y position Position of a sprite on a vertical axis

Index

Aa

abstraction 64-65,
  122-123
Aldrin, Buzz 55
algorithms 10-13, 15, 18,
  20, 80-83, 86, 116
Allen, Paul 124, 125
Altair 8800 124
Altair BASIC 124, 125
analytical engine 14-15
answers 135
Apollo 11 mission 55
arachnids 62
Arduino 131
Armstrong, Neil 55
artificial intelligence 37
astronauts 54-55
augmented reality 26

Bb

Babbage, Charles 14
backdrops 75, 79, 102
balloons 38-39
Berners-Lee, Tim 69
Bill & Melinda Gates
  Foundation 125
binary 137
biscuits 40-43
bits 137
block types 76
blocks 72, 74, 76, 77, 82,
  84, 86
Blocks Palette 74, 75, 76,
  118, 122, 132
Bombe 37
breaking loops 91
bugs 20, 85, 88-89
bytes 137

Cc

C++ 85
castle, decomposing 58-61
central processing unit
  (CPU) 44, 45
cheese biscuits 40-43
chess 37
clones 76, 106, 109, 133,
  134
coders 5, 6, 7
coding programs 86-87
collaboration 28-29, 94-95,
  126
collisions 46-47, 106-107
color change blocks 90,
  91
comic strips 64
computer science 36, 110,
  125, 136-137
computers 44-45
condition blocks 91, 98-99,
  100-101, 106, 107
conditionals 32-33, 34,
  98-99, 100-101
consoles 27, 110-111
Control blocks 76, 106
controllers 27, 132, 133
coordinates 20-21, 77
core routers 68
costumes 74, 76, 79,
  120-121, 128
creativity 24-25, 92-93
creepy-crawlies 62-63
cursor 46

Dd

dancing 34-35, 100-101
data measurements 137
debugging 20-21, 88-89,
  96, 136
decomposition 58-61,
  116-119
define blocks 112, 114,
  118, 121, 122, 123,
  126, 132
degrees 50, 97, 113, 115

delete (blocks) 74
downloading 72, 73, 132
drawing 20-21, 24-25,
  28-29, 78, 92-93, 113,
  115
drawings, debugging
  20-21
drums 22-23, 94-95

Ee

edit menu 74
Eich, Brendan 85
ENIAC (Electronic Numerica
  Integrator and Computer)
  136, 137
Enigma machine 36-37
erase all block 92, 93, 96,
  97, 113, 115, 127, 129
errors 7, 20-21, 88-89
Event blocks 76, 77,
  102-103
events 38-39, 46, 76, 80,
  91, 102-103
extension blocks 74, 76,
  112, 132

Ff

fiber-optic cables 69
file menu 73, 74
file size 137
flowcharts 80, 81, 82-83,
  86-87, 116, 117
forever loops 90, 100, 129
fortune-teller 50-53
fruit biscuits 40-43
full screen 75
function blocks 112-113,
  120, 122, 126, 132
function with parameter
  blocks 114-115, 118,
  119, 121, 123, 126
functions 50-53, 56-57,
  76, 112-113, 114-115,
  116-119, 120-121,
  122-123, 126, 132

Gg

games 26-27, 110-111
Gates, Bill 124-125
Gates, Melinda 125
Glenn, John 54
go to blocks 77
graphics card 44

Hh

ard drive 45
ardware 44-45
arvard University 125
Hello, World!" 85
de blocks 88-89, 134
ome router 69
opper, Admiral Grace
  Murray 136
uman computers 54
umanoid robots 131

i

M 137
M 360 137
then 98-99, 101
/else blocks 100-101
/else statements 34-35
gradients 40-41
put 40-43, 44, 45,
  104-105
sects 63
struments, musical 22-23,
  26-27, 94-95
teractive programs
  104-105, 126-129
ternet 6, 26-27, 68-69,
  131, 136
P (Internet Service
  Provider) 68, 69
wata Asks" 111
vata, Satoru 110-111

Jj

JavaScript 85, 130
Johnson, Katherine 54-55

Kk

key pressed? blocks 98, 99,
  100
keyboards 6, 40, 44, 98,
  104
keylogging 136

Ll

laptops 68, 69
LED lights 130, 134
Looks blocks 76

loops 22-23, 49, 57, 76,
  90-91
loops blocks 76, 90-91, 93,
  96, 97, 100, 113, 115,
  118, 119
Lovelace, Ada 14-15

Mm

mac OS 132
malware 136
Manchester Baby 137
Massachusetts Institute of
Technology (MIT) 84

matching patterns 62-63,
  120-121
mathematics 14, 36, 54-55,
  125
Matsumoto, Yukihiro 85
mazes 56-57
memory 14, 44-45, 84
messages, coded 36-37
micro:bit 130-131, 132-
  134
micro:bit Extension 132
micro:bit HEX 132
Microsoft 27, 124-125
minicomputers 6, 130-131,
  132-134
mobile connection 68
mobile gaming 27
mobile towers 68
moon landings 55
motherboard 44, 45, 137
Motion blocks 76, 77
mouse 45
mouse down? condition 98
music 22-23, 76, 94-95
Music Extension 76
My Blocks 76, 112, 114,
  118, 121, 122, 126

Nn

name blocks 112
NASA 54-55
Nintendo 27, 110-111
Nintendo DS 110, 111

Oo

Obama, Barack 125
online gaming 26-27
online safety 73
operating systems (OS) 73, 124, 125, 132
Operator blocks 76
order, algorithms 77, 81
origami 10-13
output 40-43, 44, 45, 104-105

Pp

Paint tool 78
paper chains 48-49
paper pixels 16-17
parameter path 56-57
parameters 56-57, 114-115, 117, 118, 121, 122, 123, 126
Pascal, Blaise 137
Pascaline mechanical calculator 137
pattern matching 62-63, 120-121
patterns 96-97, 113, 115, 126-129
PCs 44, 73, 124

pen tools 76, 92-93, 112-113, 114-115, 126-129
Pen Extension 76
permissions 104, 127
persistence 7, 30-31, 96-97
pixels 16-17, 77
Playstation 27
poems 66, 67
pointing, persistence 30-31
Pokémon GO 111
Presidential Medal of Freedom 125
problem-solving 6, 24, 36, 58, 62
program writing 18-19, 86-87
programming languages 84-85, 124, 130
punched cards 15
Python 84, 85, 130

Rr

RAM (random access memory) 44-45, 137
Raspberry Pi 130, 131
recipes 10, 40-43

remixing 66-67, 126-129
repeat loops 90, 91, 118
repeat until loops 91, 98, 99, 101
reset function 121
rhymes, remixing 66-67
rhythm 94-95
robots 130, 131
routers 68-69
Ruby 85

Ss

safety 4, 73
SAGE system 137
saving work 72, 73, 74
say blocks 84
scavenger hunt program 18-19
scores 108-109, 132-134
Scratch 72-83, 86-109, 112-123, 126-129, 130, 132-134
Scratch library 78
Scratch Link 132
Scratch map 75
Scratch website 72, 73
screen layout 74-75
screens 16, 44, 45
scripts 77
Scripts Area 74, 75
Sensing blocks 76, 119
sequence 80-81
sheet music 10
show blocks 88-89, 134
smartphones 27, 44, 68
sniffers 136

ongs 66, 67
ound blocks 76
ounds 74
pacecraft 54-55
peakers 45, 104, 130
peech bubbles 76, 83
prite List 75, 78, 107
prites 75, 78-79
tage 75, 79
tage List 75, 79
tamp blocks 96-97, 128
tatements 32-35, 98
tories 29, 64-65, 66, 67
troustrup, Bjarne 85
ymbols 18-19, 137

t

eamwork 28-29, 94-95
elephone exchange 68, 69
emplates 24-25
ext-based languages 84, 85
ouching color? blocks 98
ouching conditions 98, 99, 100, 104-105, 106-107
rojan horse 136

TRS-80 137
true or false 32-35, 98-99, 100-101
Turing, Alan 15, 36-37
Turing machines 36
Turing test 37
turn blocks 76
Turochamp 37
tutorials 74

Uu

underwater cables 68
Uno 131
USB cables/ports 131, 132

Vv

value, variables 48-49, 108-109
van Rossum, Guido 84
variables 48-49, 108-109, 114-115, 117-119, 132-134
Variable blocks 76
video games 26-27, 110-111
video sensing 104, 127
Video Sensing Extension 76
virtual reality 26
viruses 136
visual programming languages 84
vulnerability scanners 136

Ww

wait blocks 88, 90, 123
webcams 76, 104-105, 126-129
web pages 85
Wi-Fi 69, 131
Wii 27, 110
Windows 124, 125, 132
wires 69
World War II 36, 37
World Wide Web 69
worms 136

Xx

x and y locations 77
Xbox 27

Yy

yes-or-no questions 32-33, 52

Zz

Z3 137
zoom 75
Zuse, Konrad 137

Acknowledgments

DK would like to thank the following: Caroline Hunt for proofreading; Helen Peters for the index; Ruth Jenkinson for photography; Elisabeth Smith for the Models; the models; Anne Damerell for legal assistance.